THE
WATCH FACTORIES
OF AMERICA
PAST AND PRESENT

A COMPLETE HISTORY OF WATCHMAKING IN AMERICA, FROM
1809 TO 1888 INCLUSIVE, WITH SKETCHES OF THE
LIVES OF CELEBRATED AMERICAN WATCH-
MAKERS AND ORGANIZERS.

BY HENRY G. ABBOTT

ILLUSTRATED WITH 50 ENGRAVINGS

Copyright © 2013 Read Books Ltd.
This book is copyright and may not be
reproduced or copied in any way without
the express permission of the publisher in writing

British Library Cataloguing-in-Publication Data
A catalogue record for this book is available from the
British Library

A History of Clocks and Watches

Horology (from the Latin, Horologium) is the science of measuring time. Clocks, watches, clockwork, sundials, clepsydras, timers, time recorders, marine chronometers and atomic clocks are all examples of instruments used to measure time. In current usage, horology refers mainly to the study of mechanical timekeeping devices, whilst chronometry more broadly included electronic devices that have largely supplanted mechanical clocks for accuracy and precision in timekeeping. Horology itself has an incredibly long history and there are many museums and several specialised libraries devoted to the subject. Perhaps the most famous is the *Royal Greenwich Observatory,* also the source of the Prime Meridian (longitude 0° 0' 0"), and the home of the first marine timekeepers accurate enough to determine longitude.

The word 'clock' is derived from the Celtic words *clagan* and *clocca* meaning 'bell'. A silent instrument missing such a mechanism has traditionally been known as a timepiece, although today the words have become interchangeable. The clock is one of the oldest human interventions, meeting the need to consistently measure intervals of time shorter than the natural units: the day, the lunar month and the year. The current sexagesimal system of time measurement dates to approximately 2000 BC in Sumer. The Ancient Egyptians divided the day into two twelve-hour periods and used large obelisks to track the movement of the sun. They also developed water clocks, which had also been employed frequently by the Ancient Greeks, who called them 'clepsydrae'. The Shang Dynasty is also believed to have used the outflow water clock around the same time.

The first mechanical clocks, employing the verge escapement mechanism (the mechanism that controls the rate of a clock by advancing the gear train at regular intervals or 'ticks') with a foliot or balance wheel timekeeper (a weighted wheel that rotates back and forth, being returned toward its centre position by a spiral), were invented in Europe at around the start of the fourteenth century. They became the standard timekeeping device until the pendulum clock was invented in 1656. This remained the most accurate timekeeper until the 1930s, when quartz oscillators (where the mechanical **resonance** of a vibrating crystal is used to create an electrical signal with a very precise **frequency**) were invented, followed by atomic clocks after World War Two. Although initially limited to laboratories, the development of microelectronics in the 1960s made **quartz clocks** both compact and cheap to produce, and by the 1980s they became the world's dominant timekeeping technology in both clocks and **wristwatches**.

The concept of the wristwatch goes back to the production of the very earliest watches in the sixteenth century. Elizabeth I of England received a wristwatch from Robert Dudley in 1571, described as an arm watch. From the beginning, they were almost exclusively worn by women, while men used pocket-watches up until the early twentieth century. This was not just a matter of fashion or prejudice; watches of the time were notoriously prone to fouling from exposure to the elements, and could only reliably be kept safe from harm if carried securely in the pocket. Wristwatches were first worn by military men towards the end of the nineteenth century, when the importance of synchronizing manoeuvres during war without potentially revealing the plan to the enemy through signalling was increasingly recognized. It was clear that using pocket watches while in the heat of battle or while mounted on a horse was impractical, so officers began to strap the watches to their wrist.

The company H. Williamson Ltd., based in Coventry, England, was one of the first to capitalize on this opportunity. During the company's 1916 AGM it was noted that '...the public is buying the practical things of life. Nobody can truthfully contend that the watch is a luxury. It is said that one soldier in every four wears a wristlet watch, and the other three mean to get one as soon as they can.' By the end of the War, almost all enlisted men wore a wristwatch, and after they were demobilized, the fashion soon caught on - the British *Horological Journal* wrote in 1917 that '...the wristlet watch was little used by the sterner sex before the war, but now is seen on the wrist of nearly every man in uniform and of many men in civilian attire.' Within a decade, sales of wristwatches had outstripped those of pocket watches.

Now that clocks and watches had become 'common objects' there was a massively increased demand on clockmakers for maintenance and repair. Julien Le Roy, a clockmaker of Versailles, invented a face that could be opened to view the inside clockwork – a development which many subsequent artisans copied. He also invented special repeating mechanisms to improve the precision of clocks and supervised over 3,500 watches. The more complicated the device however, the more often it needed repairing. Today, since almost all clocks are now factory-made, most modern clockmakers *only* repair clocks. They are frequently employed by jewellers, antique shops or places devoted strictly to repairing clocks and watches.

The clockmakers of the present must be able to read blueprints and instructions for numerous types of clocks and time pieces that vary from antique clocks to modern time pieces in order to fix and make clocks or watches. The trade requires fine motor coordination as clockmakers must frequently work on devices with small gears and fine machinery, as well as an appreciation for the original art form. As is evident from this very short history of clocks and watches, over the centuries the items themselves have changed – almost out of recognition, but the importance of time-keeping has not. It is an area which provides a constant source of fascination and scientific discovery, still very much evolving today. We hope the reader enjoys this book.

PREFACE.

FROM time immemorial it has been the custom to give every youngster a name, and so the author has christened this unpretentious volume "The Watch Factories of America." This little work is not intended to be elaborate or even perfect, nor does it present anything new or startling in the way of discovery, but is simply a collection of facts, recorded in presentable shape, in connection with the rise and development of one of the most marvelous growths of mechanical genius of this wonder-working nineteenth century.

Within the memory of yet active workers at the trade, this branch of industry has grown from the humble factory of Luther Goddard, with its weekly product of two watches, to the mammoth Waltham and Elgin factories, with their daily output of as many thousands, of the finest productions of mechanical precision as the world has ever seen. Surely such a developement deserves a history, and whether or not I have succeeded in giving it, I leave you, gentle reader, to decide. One thing is certain, that from the "Nuremburg Egg," to the last novelty in watch making, whatever that may be, the past fifty years of the nineteenth century, in our own favored land, has more than surpassed the endeavors of the intervening centuries, with all the glorious achievements of the fine workers of England, France and Switzerland; they originated, but the Yankee developed and multiplied, and has "waxed exceedingly great" in the art of modern horology.

THE AUTHOR.

CONTENTS.

CHAPTER.		PAGE.
I.	AARON L. DENNISON - - - - -	9
II.	LUTHER GODDARD. PITKIN BROS. THE AMERICAN HOROLOGE COMPANY. THE WARREN MFG. COMPANY. N. B. SHERWOOD. THE AMERICAN WALTHAM WATCH COMPANY -	15
III.	THE NASHUA WATCH COMPANY - -	33
IV.	EDWARD HOWARD. E. HOWARD WATCH AND CLOCK COMPANY - - - - -	37
V.	THE NEWARK WATCH COMPANY. THE CORNELL WATCH COMPANY - - - -	45
VI.	THE UNITED STATES WATCH COMPANY OF N. J. THE MARION WATCH COMPANY -	51
VII.	THE ELGIN NATIONAL WATCH COMPANY -	55
VIII.	J. C. ADAMS - - - - - - -	67
IX.	THE TREMONT AND MELROSE WATCH COMPANIES - - - - - - -	69
X.	THE MOZART WATCH COMPANY OF PROVIDENCE. THE NEW YORK WATCH COMPANY	71
XI.	THE MOZART WATCH COMPANY OF ANN ARBOR. THE ROCK ISLAND WATCH COMPANY. THE FREEPORT WATCH COMPANY -	75
XII.	THE ILLINOIS WATCH COMPANY - -	79
XIII.	THE ROCKFORD WATCH COMPANY - - -	83
XIV.	THE ADAMS & PERRY WATCH MFG. COMPANY. THE LANCASTER WATCH COMPANY. THE KEYSTONE WATCH COMPANY - -	85
XV.	THE FITCHBURG WATCH COMPANY - -	91
XVI.	THE AUBURNDALE WATCH COMPANY - -	93

CHAPTER.		PAGE.
XVII.	THE HAMPDEN WATCH COMPANY - - -	97
XVIII.	THE WATERBURY WATCH COMPANY - -	101
XIX.	INDEPENDENT WATCH COMPANY. FREDONIA WATCH COMPANY - - - - -	109
XX.	THE BOWMAN WATCH - - - - -	113
XXI.	COLUMBUS WATCH COMPANY - - - -	115
XXII.	AURORA WATCH COMPANY - - - -	119
XXIII.	TRENTON WATCH COMPANY - - - -	123
XXIV.	CHARLES S. MOSELEY. P. S. BARTLETT -	127
XXV.	CHESHIRE WATCH COMPANY. MANHATTAN WATCH COMPANY - - - - - -	133
XXVI.	THE SELF WINDING WATCH. THE UNITED STATES WATCH COMPANY OF WALTHAM	137
XXVII.	THE PEORIA WATCH COMPANY. THE N. Y. STANDARD, SETH THOMAS AND WICHITA COMPANIES - - - - - - -	141

THE
WATCH FACTORIES
OF AMERICA.

THE term watchmaker, in America, does not necessarily imply one who manufactures watches, but is more generally applied to those who make a business of repairing and cleaning time pieces. In days gone by, a watchmaker was a mechanic of no mean order, capable of making and fitting any part of a watch, no matter what make the watch might have been or how complicated its construction, which through negligence on the part of the owner became deranged or broken. To-day, a watchmaker need be possessed of only ordinary mechanical skill and intelligence in order to repair any watch of American manufacture, and all this change has come about by the manufacturers of the various movements working on the interchangeable system, first applied to watchmaking in America by Mr. Aaron L. Dennison in 1850.

AARON L. DENNISON.

Aaron L. Dennison was the son of a shoemaker of Freeport, Me. He was born in the year 1812, and in 1822 we find him carrying a mason's hod in the village of Topsham. In 1825 we find him earning his own living, though but thirteen years of age, by sawing wood in the town of Brunswick, his father having removed to the latter place in 1824. Two years later he might have been found working at his father's trade. At eighteen years of age he began to grow tired of cobbling. He was of a mechanical turn of mind and was much interested in watchmaking and kindred mechanical work, and his father recognizing this fact apprenticed him to James Carey, a watchmaker of Brunswick, in 1830. In 1833 he left Brunswick, to perfect himself as a journeyman watchmaker, entering the employ of Currier & Trot, of Boston. Shortly after, he went into business for himself, but soon gave it up to enter the employ of Messrs. Jones, Low & Ball. While at work here he received the benefit of the advice of Mr. Tubal Hone, then considered one of the finest watchmakers in the country; and it was here in the year 1835 that Mr. Dennison discovered the inaccuracies of workmanship and construction which existed in even the best of hand-made watches. In a letter written at that time he said: " Within a year I have examined watches made by a man whose reputation at this moment is far beyond that of any other watchmaker in London, and have found in them such workmanship as I should blush to have it supposed had passed from under my hands in our lower grade of work. Of course I do not mean to say that there is not work in these watches of the highest grade possible to carry the finisher's art, but errors do creep in and are allowed to pass the hands of competent examiners, and it needs but slight acquaintance with our art to discover that the lower grade of foreign watches are hardly as mechanically correct in their construction as a common wheelbarrow."

From Boston he went to New York city, but in 1839 we again find him in Boston, in business for himself. Here he did repairing for the trade and carried a line of tools and materials. A few years later we find him carrying a full line of watches and jewelry and doing a thriving business. About this time he invented the " Dennison Standard

Gauge," and began to turn his thoughts upon the manufacture of watches on what is now known as the "Interchangeable System."

We will here use Mr. Dennison's own words:

"The principal thinking up of the matter was done when I was in business at the corner of Bromfield and Washington Streets, Boston; and many a night after I had done a good day's work at the store and a good evening's work at home, in repairing watches for personal friends, I used to stroll out upon the common and give my mind full play upon this project; and now, as far as I can recollect what my plans then were as to system and methods to be employed, they were identical with those in existence at the principal watch factories at the present time."*

Mr. Dennison predicted, in the year 1846, that within twenty years the manufacture of watches would be reduced to as much system and perfection and with the same expedition that fire-arms were then made in the Springfield armory. He often visited this armory and took great interest in examining the various processes of finishing fire-arms.

In 1849 a friend of Mr. Dennison, Mr. Edward Howard, a clock and scale maker of Boston, had a long talk with him in regard to the manufacture of American locomotives. Mr. Dennison did not agree with Mr. Howard in his idea of locomotive manufacture, but soon convinced him that the manufacture of watches, in large quantities on the interchangeable plan, would prove a more profitable undertaking. Mr. Howard soon became as enthusiastic over the idea as Mr. Dennison and together they went in search of a capitalist who was willing to risk some money in the experiment. This gentleman was found in the person of Mr. Samuel Curtis, of Boston, who furnished

---

*Dr. Leonard Waldo's address, delivered before the Society of Arts, London, May 19, 1886.

$20,000 with which to try the experiment. Mr. Howard's partner, Mr. D. P. Davis, was also interested in the experiment. The projectors met together at an early date to make arrangements in regard to the starting of the factory and buying the necessary material. We will again quote from Mr. Dennison's own words:

"I suggested that the first money spent in the undertaking should be for a tour of observation in the watchmaking districts in England, with the view of ascertaining whether the trade of watchmaking was carried on there on the system represented to me by English workmen I had employed from time to time in repairing. Another object I had in view was to find out the source of supply for the necessary materials, such as enamel for dials, jewels, etc."

Mr. Dennison started for Europe and after thoroughly looking over the ground, writes:

"I found that the matter had been correctly represented, but in carrying out their system one-half the truth had not been told. How that the party setting up as manufacturer of watches bought his Lancashire movements—a conglomeration of rough materials—and gave them out to A, B, C, and D to have them finished; and how A, B, C, and D, gave out the different jobs of pivoting certain wheels of the train to E, certain other parts to F, and the fusee cutting to G. Dial-making, jeweling, gilding, motioning, etc., to others, down almost the entire length of the alphabet; and how that, taking these various pieces of work to outside workpeople—who, if sober enough to be at their places, were likely to be engaged on some one's work who had been ahead of them, and how, under such circumstances, he would take the occasion to drop into a 'pub' to drink and gossip, and, perhaps, unfit himself for work the remainder of the day. Finding things in this condition as a matter of course, my theory of Americans not finding any difficulty in competing with the English, especially if the interchangeable system and manufacturing in large quantities was adopted, may be accepted as reasonable."

While Mr. Dennison was looking over the ground in Europe, Mr. Howard was engaged in erecting a factory, and on the return of Mr. Dennison, work was immediately commenced. It is not our object to follow the history of this factory just here, as it will be taken up later on, but simply to give a short sketch of Mr. Dennison's career. Suffice it to say, therefore, that the factory was built, the tools manufactured and everything started in 1851, and the first watches were placed upon the market in 1853. The company was not a financial success and they finally made an assignment in 1857. Mr. Dennison was then employed by his successors as superintendent, filling that position until December, 1861.

In 1864, Mr. Dennison interested Mr. A. O. Bigelow, of Boston, in a new factory, of which we will speak in due time. Mr. Dennison's past experience had taught him that to start a watch factory the projectors must be bountifully supplied with money, and must be prepared to sink a great deal before realizing a single dollar. Owing to the high price of labor at this time and the necessities above described, Mr. Dennison reasoned that it would be better to have certain portions of the movements made in Switzerland, imported to the United States, and set up with the remaining portions which were to be made in America.

Accordingly, Mr. Dennison went to Switzerland, and after thoroughly looking over the ground decided that Zurich was the best location. He here gathered the necessary material together, set up the trains and sent them to Boston. Everything went along swimmingly until 1866, when the directors of the company decided to build a new factory at Melrose, Mass., and make the entire watch there.

This new idea, however, Mr. Dennison did not approve of, as the company was doing very well as it was, and the change would involve more or less risk. Accordingly, in a short time after, he withdrew from the company. Mr. Dennison remained in Switzerland until 1870, having taken a contract to furnish certain material for the Melrose Company. The company having failed, Mr. Dennison returned to America and tried to interest capital in reviving it. Failing in this, however, he soon went to England, where he interested capitalists, and the plant was purchased and a factory opened. Mr. Dennison is in no way connected with this company, which is still running under the name of the "English Watch Company," but is engaged in watch case manufacturing in Birmingham, where it is said he is doing a thriving business.

CHAPTER II.

IT would be a very hard thing to determine just who the first manufacturer of watches in America was, since in the beginning of the nineteenth century many of the trade manufactured movements in small quantities, either to order or for the purpose of carrying in stock until such time as a purchaser might turn up. These watches were of necessity hand-made, and the manufacturers depended considerably upon Europe for supplies, such as hands, springs, jewels, balances, etc.

In 1809, Luther Goddard, of Shrewsbury, Mass., commenced to manufacture watches of the verge pattern, in somewhat larger quantities than had been attempted before. Mr. Goddard could not compete with the cheap foreign watches, however, and retired from the business in 1817, having manufactured about 500 watches. This was the greatest number of watches ever made by any one manufacturer in America up to this time.

Following closely in the wake of Mr. Goddard, in 1812, an establishment for the manufacture of watches was started in Worcester, Mass. The establishment was small, and was suspended shortly after for want of ready funds. In 1838 the first machine-made watch ever made in America was placed upon the market. It was known as the Pitkin watch, and was manufactured by two brothers, James and Henry Pitkin, at Hartford, Conn. These movements were three-quarter plate, slow train and about the diameter of the modern 16-size. The machinery used in their manufacture was very crude, and was all made by the Pitkin Bros. The Pitkin watch, however, fared the same fate as its predecessors. The cost of manufacture was too great to compete with those made by the Swiss, and shortly after moving the factory to New York, which they did in 1841, the idea was abandoned. The total product of the Pitkins was about 800 movements.

Following Pitkin Bros., came several other small manufacturers, but nothing important in this line was attempted until the year 1849, when the nucleus of what is now known as the American Waltham Watch Company was established.

A person standing on Crescent street, Waltham, and gazing upon the mammoth structure occupied by the American Waltham Watch Company as a factory, a building whose frontage occupies nearly 700 feet, within whose walls 2,800 workmen are daily employed, and from which 7,500 time-keepers are turned out weekly, can scarcely realize that the company has seen failure and disaster staring them in the face on more than one occasion; but such is a fact. The road to success is not always strewn with roses, and although the company is now one of the largest of its kind in the world, yet it has struggled with adversity, and has seen the time when, we might say, the toss of a penny would have decided whether they would continue, or give up in despair.

In the fall of the year, 1849, Mr. Dennison commenced to build machinery for the manufacture of watches on the interchangeable system, having associated himself with Howard & Davis, as described in the previous chapter. A small room was divided off in Howard & Davis' factory, and there Mr. Dennison commenced work on his machines. In 1850 a small factory was built opposite Howard & Davis' shop, and some English and Swiss watchmakers put to work. Mr. Dennison's machinery was not a success, however, and one of Howard & Davis' men was detailed to help Mr. Dennison, and after numerous attempts, they finally succeeded in getting together a few tools and machines of anything but perfect construction.

In the summer of 1850, Mr. Dennison completed the model of the first watch, which corresponded with the full plate 18-size of to-day. This watch was made to run eight days, but proved to be a failure, and its place was filled by a one-day watch. At this time the firm was known as "The American Horologe Company," and consisted of A. L Dennison, E. Howard, D. P. Davis and Sam'l Curtis. Mr. Curtis took no active part in the management of the concern, but furnished most of the money with which the buildings and machinery were built. After a lapse of about one year the name of the company was changed to "The Warren Manufacturing Company," and the first hundred watches bore that name. The first watches were actually placed upon the market in 1853. The name "Samuel Curtis" was substituted for "Warren" on the next six or seven hundred watches, the reason being that the name, "The Warren Manufacturing Company," was abandoned as being unfitting, and the name, "Boston Watch Company" was used instead. These watches were 18-size, full plate, slow train and were sold at $40.

In 1853 Mr. Dennison became dissatisfied with the location of the factory, as it was very dusty in summer and proper accomodations for the dwellings of the employes could not be obtained. He visited Waltham and looked over the land at Stony Brook, trying to purchase from Mr. Sibley a tract of land, which is now occupied in part by N. L. Sibley's machine shop, a spot which attracted the attention of Mr. Dennison by its romantic scenery and its location, being out of the regular line of travel. Failing to make terms with Mr. Sibley, he called upon a friend, Mr. S. P.

Emerson, who at that time was in the machine shop of the Boston Manufacturing Company, and to whom he confided the object of his visit. Mr. Emerson suggested the Bemis farm as being in the market and a suitable site. The land was examined and found desirable, and Mr. Emerson subsequently introduced Mr. Dennison to prominent citizens of Waltham, who became interested and took hold of the matter, until on March 24, 1854, " The Waltham Improvement Company" was incorporated by special act of the legislature, with a capital stock of $100,000, " The Boston Watch Company" owning thirty shares of $100 each. The building for the watch factory was started at once, and was ready for occupancy October 5, 1854. At this time the company was making about five watches per day, and employed about ninety hands.

After removing to Waltham, the movements were engraved " Dennison, Howard and Davis." About this time Mr. Howard made the acquaintance of Mr. N. B. Sherwood, who then resided in New York City, and placed him in charge of the jeweling department. We will here deviate from the subject long enough to give a short sketch of the life of Mr. Sherwood, who was one of the most remarkable and able mechanics ever connected with a watch factory.

NAPOLEON BONAPARTE SHERWOOD.

Mr. Sherwood was born in 1823, was educated in Albany Academy, under Prof. Beck, and graduated with high honors. From a boy he was passionately fond of mathematics, astronomy and chemistry, and was a born mechanical genius. After graduating from Albany Academy he decided to practice medicine, and no young man ever gave more brilliant promise of becoming eminent in that profession. For some reason he suddenly took a dislike to the calling, and through the influence of a friend, who was a dentist, he engaged in that profession for a time, and was one of the first to realize that the old crucibles thrown away by dentists contained a great deal of gold. At that time all plates were made of gold or silver. He was anxious to see more of the world, so he traveled westward. He was accompanied by his dentist friend, and when their money gave out they would stop in some town a few weeks and would soon have all the work they could do, as Mr. Sherwood was a fine talker and had no trouble in securing patronage. When work slacked up they would resume their travels, and they finally landed in Chicago. They soon ran short of money and not being able to secure any dental work, Mr. Sherwood entered the office of an engineer and soon secured a position as draughtsman, and shortly after was put in charge of a surveying corps and made a survey for a railroad. His friend was one of the chain bearers. He soon had money enough to resume his travels, when he and his friend pushed on southward.

Finally their money again gave out and Mr. Sherwood secured a position as draughtsman in the office of a machine shop, getting a position for his friend in the shop. He finally drifted to Pennsylvania, where he opened a drug store. While engaged in the drug business he took up the study of watchmaking. About this time he married Miss Mary Van Valkenburg. His drug store venture not proving a success, he gave it up and went to Jefferson, a small village in Ashtabula County, Ohio, where he opened a watchmaker's shop, also taking a class in the higher mathematics in the school there. He made a good support for his family but could lay up no money, so in the spring of 1853, at the solicitation of some of his friends, he opened a machine shop. He made his own drawings, and when his blacksmith would get on a spree he would do his own forging. Jefferson proved to be too small a place for a watchmaker or machine shop, so about 1855 he went to New York, where he engaged as a traveling salesman for a notion house, and on one of his home visits made the acquaintance of Mr. Willson, a son-in-law of Mr. Curtis, and by him was invited to visit Waltham and the watch factory, with the hope that he could be induced to remain there. Seeing the opening for the exercise of his talents in mechanics, this was no difficult matter, and on the other hand Mr. Howard saw in him the material his firm needed.

A gentleman well acquainted with Mr. Sherwood, recently said: "He was a wonderful man; a thorough mechanic, gifted with the highly retentive memory and perceptive powers that seemed almost intuitive. He had the faculty of being able to grasp any subject of mechanics which was brought to his notice, and his fertile brain and faculty for imparting information, made him an interesting companion and valuable writer and instructor. Unlike other mechanics and inventors, he seemed to grasp the whole idea and work out his problem almost instantaneous."

His connection with the Waltham factory gave him abundant opportunity to bring his inventive genius into play in originating new tools to do work formerly done by hand. He not only conceived new ideas, but being an excellent draughtsman, he placed them on paper, and then entering the machine shop, he, with his own hands, made and put them together.

Under his charge the jeweling department soon made a complete revolution. New systems and methods of doing work were introduced, new machines made and the amount of work turned out was doubled. Many of the tools used to-day in our watch factories were invented and first built by Mr. Sherwood. A list and description of the various tools invented by this remarkable man would fill a good

N. B. SHERWOOD.

sized volume, and we will confine our remarks to but a few of them. He invented what is known as the "Countersinker or screw head tool," for jewel screws; "The End-shake Tools;" The Opener" and " The Truing-up Tools." "The End-shake Tools," were truly wonderful machines, being self-measuring and so constructed that no matter to what depth the shoulder was cut in the upper plates, by putting the plate against one end of one of the tools, and the jewel with its setting in a spring chuck the tool would cut a shoulder on the setting that would bring the face of each and every jewel exactly flush with the under side of the plate when the setting was put in. The jewels were then reversed and put into another chuck and the top of the setting cut down by this magic tool until it would come exactly flush with the top of the plate, or rather leave just enough projecting above to allow for polishing. After the jewel settings were "stripped" or polished, they were put into the plates where they belonged never to be removed again. As the plate was already gilded, next the holes for the screws were tapped out and the holes bored for each screw-head on the screw-head tool, that would leave the head of the screw exactly flush with the top of the plate and not raise any burr. The end-shake tool was certainly the perfection of self-measuring tools. By it the shoulder was cut on the setting of the lower holes, (the holes in the plate being first bored out with a shoulder), so as to give each pinion and staff the exact amount of end-shake required. With these tools one man could do nicer work and more of it than any five men could do in the ordinary way.

The so-called "Opener" was another ingenious tool. Mr. Sherwood found that it was impossible to open a jewel hole by hand so that the hole would be absolutely round, and accordingly he produced a tool which would do the work not only perfectly but rapidly. He never patented any of his inventions, for he never took a pecuniary view of the value of them. His whole purpose and life was devoted to perfecting the article or tool he had in hand, and when that was accomplished, he was ready for something else. Many of his inventions can be found in daily use in the watch factories of the United States to-day. Some of the minor details of these machines have been improved on, but in many cases no improvements have been made in the machines, as orginally built by him, as far back as 1860.

Mr. Sherwood left the employ of Mr. Howard in the fall of 1858, to go into business with Mr. James Queen, in New York City. The death of his wife, which occured in the spring of 1859, played sad havoc with him. She left him with two children, both girls. The youngest child died when an infant and the eldest was cared for by the mother's relatives. She married Mr. David Botsford, of Adrian, Mich., and is now living in Allen, Mich. Shortly after the death of his wife, Mr. Sherwood became restless and dissatisfied. In the summer of 1859 he dissolved partnership with Mr. Queen and went to Cleveland, Ohio, where he entered the employ of Mr. Crittenden. In the fall of 1859, he left Cleveland and returned to New York. He then went to Perth Amboy, N. J., where he started a small shop and did fairly well. He was very desirous of enlisting in the civil war, but his poor health prevented him doing so.

In 1864, Mr. Sherwood interested capitalists and organized the "Newark Watch Company." A misunderstanding occurred, however, in a few months and Mr. Sherwood retired. He died of consumption in New York City, in October, 1872, in his 40th year. He was of a generous nature, always ready to help the poor, and he would deny himself a meal or a coat any day of his life, to feed and clothe a mendicant. In his prosperous days he always carried a pocketfull of pennies which he would distribute among the streetarabs whom he might meet. Mr. Sherwood was an able writer and his articles, which appeared in *The American Horological Journal*, were read with great interest by the trade.

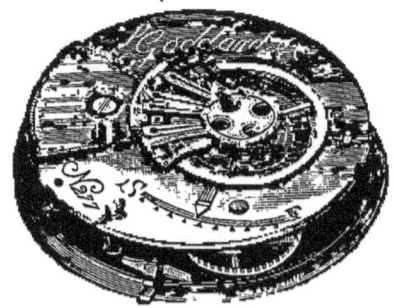

THE GODDARD WATCH.

Mr. Sherwood was a man who possessed more general information than falls to the lot of most men. He was up on all scientific subjects, and kept up with the current literature of the day. Anything pertaining to mathematics had a charm for him; he delighted in difficult algebraic problems, was a rapid reader, and could read, and take in ten pages to any ordinary person's one. He never forgot what he read or heard. He could read a description of a city that he had never seen, and long afterwards give a detailed account of the streets, homes and noted people.

We will now revert back to our original subject, the American Watch Company, which we left to give the foregoing sketch of Mr. Sherwood.

The fall of 1856 found the watch company in desperate circumstances. All the ready money of the company had been expended, and the sales of watches were very slow. Matters went from

THE PITKIN WATCH.

bad to worse, until the spring of 1857, when the company made an assignment. The assignee offered the property for sale, and it was bid in by Mr. Royal E. Robbins for $56,500, for himself and the firm of Tracy & Baker, of Philadelphia, who were creditors of the defunct company, having furnished them with cases. The property consisted of the real estate, factory, and numerous other buildings, the machinery, steam engine, shafting, etc., together with the material unmanufactured and in process of manufacture.

THE WALTHAM FACTORY IN 1857.

The new firm was known as Tracy, Baker & Co., but Mr. Baker having a case business to look after, and having had a good offer made him by Mr. Robbins, decided to sell out his interest. Mr. Robbins then associated himself with Mr. James Appleton, and the firm was known as Appleton, Tracy & Co. The winter of 1857 proved a rough one for the new company. Money was scarce and times hard, and in the spring following Mr. Robbins about made up his mind to remove the factory nearer to New York, which was then the market for his goods. He finally made the Improvement Company a proposition to consolidate, which was accepted, the Watch Company being put in at $225,000 and the Improvement Company at $75,000. The consolidation took place in the summer of 1858. Early in the year 1859 the name of the company was changed to the American Watch Company, with a capital stock of $300,000, Mr. Robbins being elected treasurer and general business manager.

John J. Lynch went to work for the Boston Watch Company in May, 1852, and when the factory was removed to

AMERICAN WALTHAM WATCH COMPANY'S FACTORY.

Waltham in 1854 he was employed in the jeweling room. For thirty-one years and up to the time of his death, Sept. 14, 1885, he was a trusted and valuable employe of the Waltham Company. He was a thorough mechanic and understood perfectly the system of machine watch making. He was born in New York City, Nov. 10, 1830, being at the time of his death in his fifty-fifth year.

Alonzo Noble, the present foreman of the plate room, went to work for the company March 17, 1859.

In the fall of the year 1859 several of the best workmen in the Waltham factory were induced to join forces with a new factory just started in Nashua, N. H., which we will speak of in due time.

Mr. Ambrose Webster, now of the American Watch Tool Co., Waltham, who was up to this time a workman in the machine shop, was promoted to the position of mechanical superintendent, a position which he filled with great credit for many years. When he took charge of the machine shop it was as crude as could well be imagined. There was absolutely no system, no appreciation of the fact that the machine shop was the foundation of the manufactory. The proprietors did not seem to realize that to successfully run a factory they must have some persons outside of watch repairers. Anything approaching an automatic machine was frowned upon.

"CRESCENT STREET" MOVEMENT.

In spite of this fact, Mr. Webster forced automatic machinery to the front and constructed a machine to run half automatically against the positive orders of the management. He also reduced the unsystematic method of measurement, then employed in the factory, to a system, having found that there were nine classes of measuring units or gauges, which he changed for one. He designed, and George Hunter, (now superintendent of the Elgin Company's factory), built the first watch factory lathe with hard spindles and bearings, of the two-taper variety. He also made the first interchangeable standard for parts of lathes. The management was soon

"RIVERSIDE VIEW" REAR OF THE AMERICAN WALTHAM WATCH COMPANY'S FACTORY.

forced to recognize that good mechanics were more essential as heads of departments than watchmakers, and that the head machinist was, or should be, the most essential man in the factory. He invented many machines now in use in the factory, conspicuous among them being an "Automatic Pinion Cutter" invented by him in 1865. In 1872 he was made assistant superintendent, a position which he filled until his resignation, in 1876.

In 1860 the American Watch Company declared a dividend of five per cent., this being the first dividend declared by any watch factory in America. The first ladies' watch ever manufactured in America, was turned out by the company in 1861, and was known as the "P. S. Bartlett," and was a 10-size, key wind. In 1862 the American Watch Company purchased the plant of the Nashua Watch Company, of Nashua, N. H., organized in 1859, and of which we will speak in another chapter. An addition was made to the American Watch Factory, and the machinery and help were transfered from Nashua to this building. From this time on, the prosperity of the company was assured. Dividends were declared yearly, the greatest of which, in 1865, was 210 per cent. In this year, Mr. Robbins paid personally, an income tax on $337,000, the largest income in the city of Boston. The capital stock of the company was increased to $1,500,000 in 1872. In 1878 many additions and improvements were made in the factory. Wings were built on and departments enlarged, until in 1882 scarcely a vestige was left of the old factory. In 1877 the first chronographs were made; in 1883 the first split seconds. In 1871 the firm erected in Bond St., New York, what was known as the Waltham Building, which contained the general offices of the company and their gold case works. This building was destroyed by fire in 1877, and the building at present occupied by the firm was built shortly after. This company received the highest award at the Centennial Exposition, 1876; Paris, 1878; Sidney, 1879; Melbourne, 1880, and Inventions Exhibition in London, 1885. In 1885 the capital stock of the company was increased to $2,000,000, and the name changed to the American Waltham Watch Company, under which title it still continues.

In the fall of 1885, Mechanical Superintendent Marsh invented an automatic lathe that is now in successful operation, turning out 12,000 jewel settings a day.

The various positions in the factory are at present occupied as follows: E. C. Fitch, superintendent; Mr. Shirley, assistant superintendent; Leonard Green, foreman plate room; Wm. H. Wrenn, foreman machine shop; Martin Thomas, foreman train room; Alfred Warren, foreman of jeweling room; J. N. Hammond, foreman finishing and repairing departments; J. L. Keyser, foreman balance room; H. M. Haines, foreman 18-size finishing room; Joseph Bates, foreman adjusting room; Thomas Gill, foreman three-quarter plate finishing room; H. N. Fisher, foreman 'scape room; Wm. Murray, foreman engraving room; J. T. Shepherd, foreman flat steel department; Charles Berlin, foreman nickel finishing; W. R. Wills, foreman jewel making; E. U. Hull, foreman dial painting; N. P. Mulloy, foreman hand making; Charles Moore, foreman dial making; Alonzo Noble, foreman plate room; Charles H. Mann, foreman screw making; Charles B. Hicks, foreman gilding room; John Logan, main-springs, springing of balances and hairsprings; D. O'Hara, foreman case rooms; Charles J. Olney, superintendent of buildings; J. C. Sawin, carpenter.

CHAPTER III.

IN the last chapter we mentioned the fact that the American Watch Company purchased the plant of the Nashua Watch Company in 1868, and to this company, which was short lived, we will now call your attention.

Owing to the supposed success which Mr. Dennison had in the manufacture of watches by machinery, the attention of jewelers and capitalists throughout the United States was called to the industry as a good investment. Mr. B. D. Bingham, of Nashua, N. H., a manufacturer of clocks and regulators in a small way, went to Waltham and entered the employ of the company, being desirous of learning the modus operandi of watch manufacturing.

At this time N. P. Stratton was assistant superintendent of the Waltham company, and being of an ambitious turn of mind, was desirous of manufacturing a watch of better quality than that manufactured at Waltham. Messrs. Bingham and Stratton became fast friends and devoted much of their time while out of the factory in talking over the prospects of a watch factory, should one be organized in Nashua. Mr. Bingham felt certain that he could interest capitalists in the scheme, and accordingly with a view of doing so, and looking over the ground, Messrs. Stratton and Bingham visited Nashua in 1859. L. W. Noyes and others approved of the idea, furnished capital, and a company was formed that fall. The capital stock of the company was $100,000, with L. W. Noyes as treasurer, V. C. Gilman, president, and T. W. Lovell, secretary. A suitable building was purchased and altered over to meet the necessities of a watch factory. Mr. Stratton returned to Waltham and succeeded in employing several of the company's best men, among whom may be mentioned, C. V. Woerd, Ira G. Blake, Chas. S. Moseley, who was first or master mechanic, and Jas. H. Gerry. The loss of these gentlemen was a severe blow to the Waltham company.

Mr. Stratton was a decidedly intellectual and skillful workman, having served his time under Henry and James Pitkin, in their Hartford factory, and was afterward in the employ of the Boston Watch Company. He entered the employ of the Waltham company in 1852, and was sent to Coventry, Eng., by that institution, to learn the secret and art of etching and gilding movements; In 1857 he was made assistant superintendent of the Waltham factory, and in 1858 invented and patented a main-spring barrel, and later a hair-spring stud, both of which were adopted by the Waltham company. Mr. Stratton was not only a thorough mechanic, but was also an excellent business man; he opened the London office of the Waltham Watch Company in 1874.

James H. Gerry was also an able mechanic who thorougly understood escapement making. He afterward became superintendent of the United States Watch Company, and left that institution to become superintendent of the New York Watch Company. Later on he became superintendent of the Howard Watch and Clock Company, which position he filled until 1877. He was also inventer and patentee of a stem-wind attachment, which after modification, was adopted by the Howard company. He went into the clock manufacturing business in Elgin, and in 1885 went to Brooklyn, N. Y., to act as superintendent of the National Clock Company.

J. B. Gooding invented the capsule method of making balances still used by the factories.

Chas. S. Moseley's name will always be mentioned in connection with American watch manufacture as the designer and inventor of some of the most delicate, complicated and ingenious machinery used in the construction of a watch. He was originally a machinist and master mechanic for the Boston Watch Company at Roxbury, and was early connected with the Waltham company. He went to Elgin in 1864 to act as superintendent, a position which he occupied until May, 1872. He also occupied at different times the position of machine shop and 18-size train room foreman in the Waltham factory. He invented a large portion of the machinery, tools and improvements now used by the Elgin company, among which may be mentioned the " compound chuck " and " improved hair-spring stud."

Mr. C. V. Woerd invented the celebrated automatic pinion cutter in 1864. In 1869 he modeled the Waltham company's " Crescent Street " movement; in 1874 he invented the automatic screw machine, which attracted so much attention at the Centennial Exposition in Philadelphia and the Inventions Exhibition in London; he became superintendent of the Waltham factory in 1876, which position he filled with credit until his resignation in 1883.

Mr. Chas. S. Moseley, upon his arrival in Nashua, immediately proceeded to design and build the necessary machinery, and it was this machinery that enabled the company to construct a watch of superior grade and merit, and which was subsequently moved at the time of the sale to Waltham, and with it chiefly the watches bearing the trade marks of " American Watch Company " and "Appleton, Tracy & Co." were made. The movements were 16 and 20-size, key-wind, three-quarter plate, with exposed pallets and expansion balance.

The company had about thirty employes, Mr. Stratton acting as superintendent, C. V. Woerd as foreman of train room, J. H. Gerry, as foreman of 'scape room, Chas. S. Moseley, as master machanic, Jas. Gooding, foreman of balance making, Jas. Fairchild, foreman gilding room, Ira G. Blake foreman plate room, Frank Robbins, foreman jeweling room, J. Moorehouse, foreman dial room, and B. D. Bingham, master watchmaker. In 1862 the company running short of money, and the stockholders refusing to pay assessments, the company came to a stand still; it was finally decided that the best thing they could do was to sell the plant if a customer could be found. Accordingly, Mr. Stratton went to Boston, and entered into negotiations with Mr. R. E. Robbins, which resulted in the Waltham concern purchasing the plant for $53,000. Mr. C. W. Fogg was sent to Nashua to take charge of the factory until the fall of 1862, when the plant was moved to Waltham. The Nashua company up to the time of the sale had manufactured about 1,000 movements, none of which had ever been put upon the market, not being completed; they were afterward completed and sold as Waltham movements.

CHAPTER IV.

MR. EDWARD HOWARD, the veteran watch and clock-maker of Boston, was born in Hingham, Mass., Oct. 6, 1813. He is a practical man, having served a regular apprenticeship at the trade of clockmaking. At the age of twenty-nine he entered into partnership with D. P. Davis in the manufacture of clocks and regulators. Their business was a flourishing one, and they soon earned a reputation for turning out clocks, second to none in the country. Mr. Howard was of a mechanical turn of mind, and a list of his inventions would fill a small volume Among his various inventions was that very important piece of mechanism, the "Swing Rest." The amount of labor saved by this machine and the quality of work done would seem to be enough to make Mr. Howard's name famous among watchmakers. The greatest tribute that we can pay to Mr. Howard for his services to the horological world is to quote the words of a man who was fully capable of judging of the worth of his inventions from a practical standpoint, one who had worked under him for years and knew his sterling worth both as a fellow workman and a

THE HOWARD WATCH.

master, one who has gone to his long rest—N. B. Sherwood. He said: * " The firmness, sagacity, and almost intuitive knowledge of mechanics that he possesses will not be fully understood for years; and yet to no one man are the United States so much indebted, in so far as the manufacture of watches is concerned. We remember the dark days of its history, when the infant was unable to walk, when everything was to be created; even those who were to do the work had to be educated. But it was not so easy a task to navigate the watch factory through the stormy financial seas. In the mechanical parts, however, Mr. Howard was triumphant; not that he invented even a tithe of the processes and tools, but he had the sagacity to appreciate the value of any plan which might be submitted, and he had the firmness to carry out the idea, in the face of all the opposition of those who should have aided—indeed, of the absolute treachery of those in his employ. We do not assert that he was the entirety of the watchmaking, but we will assert that he has done more than any other one man to bring the watch manufacture to its present high standing in this country."

Immediately after the sale of the Waltham factory to Mr. Royal E. Robbins, in 1857, Mr. Howard returned to Roxbury and continued his clock business in connection with Mr. Davis; but he still had a longing after the watchmaking business, and soon opened up the old factory of the " Boston Watch Company," in Roxbury, with a small force. About one year after starting, Mr. Howard was able to place his product upon the market. They were 18-size, three-quarter plate, and were the first quick-train movements ever made in this country. Even in those early days of American watchmaking, the Howard watches were noted for their superior qualities as time-keepers; a reputation which followed them up to the present time. In order to increase the working capital of the company, a stock company was

---

*Watch and Chronometer Jeweling by N. B. Sherwood, written in Oct. 1869.

EDWARD HOWARD.

organized in 1861, with a capital of $120,000, and was known as the "Howard Clock and Watch Company." The new company struggled against adversity until the spring of 1863, when it was decided that the factory should be sold to the highest bidder and the indebtedness paid off.

A buyer, however, was not readily found, and in the following fall a new company was organized under the name of "The Howard Watch and Clock Company," with a capital of $120,000. Mr. E. Howard was elected President of this company. Several improvements were made by the new company.

The entire product of the company was controlled by a syndicate of New York jobbers from 1863 until 1870, when the company decided to establish their own agency in New York.

The first nickel movement was placed on the market in 1871, and the year following the first ladies' watch made its appearance. In 1881, the E. Howard Watch and Clock Company succeeded the old company, the capital being placed at $250,000. In 1882, Mr. Howard severed his connection with the watch company. He has retired from all active business and still resides in Boston.

The various offices and positions in the factory are occupied as follows: Samuel Little, president; Albert Howard, general superintendent; Charles J. Hayden, treasurer; C. V. Clerque, N. Y. agent; Harry Howard, Chicago agent; W. B. Learned, superintendent; T. H. Sloan, foreman finishing dep't.; A. Horton and Henry Allen, adjusting; J. R. Howard, motion; Wm. Walden and A. L. McIntosh, escapement; E. F. Emery, stem winding; A. B. Winston, screw; Alfred Barton, gliding and damaskeening; Wm. Howarth, engraving; Henry Smidt, jewel making; Chas. Chase, jeweling; Josiah Moorhouse, dial; Orin R. Dickey, balance; H. E. Fay, pinion forwarding; L. B.

THE E. HOWARD WATCH & CLOCK COMPANY'S WATCH FACTORY.

Ranlett, pinion finishing; Wm. Norton, plate; John Holden, flat steel; Wm. Bradford, spring making; C. E. Ward, springing; W. B. Hammond, inspecting.

This company employs about one hundred hands in the watch department, and the output is about 450 movements per month.

CHAPTER V.

IN 1863, Mr. N. B. Sherwood went to New York to try and interest capital in the organization of a watch factory. Messrs. Louis S. Fellows & Schell became interested in the idea and decided to try the experiment. A room was rented and Mr. Sherwood started building the machinery for the new enterprise. He had under him a corps of efficient workmen, but after a few months some misunderstanding arose, and Mr. Arthur Wadsworth succeeded him.

THE NEWARK WATCH.

Messrs. Fellows & Schell purchased a building in Newark, N. J., and altered it over to serve as a factory. The machinery and tools were moved into it in 1864, and the name, "The Newark Watch Company" was adopted. The parties interested were Augustus, Robert and Edward Schell, and Lewis S. Fellows. The original model was made by Mr. Wadsworth, and was 18-size, and closely resembled an English watch then on the market. The first watches were finished in 1867. These watches were all key-wind; but later on a stem-wind movement was made, but was pronounced a failure. The movements were called, "Robert Fellows," "Edward Bevin," and

"Newark Watch Company." The stem-wind was named, "The Arthur Wadsworth," after the inventor. The company manufactured in all about 3,000 watches, but was gradually running behind. Accordingly, in 1869, negotiations were entered into with the Cornell Watch Company, then organizing at Chicago.

Mr. Paul Cornell, after whom the new factory was named, was a wealthy real-estate dealer of Chicago, owning large tracts of land in the vicinity of Grand Crossing, a few miles south of Chicago. He conceived the idea that a watch factory would be a good speculation, and if located on his property would " boom " its sale. In company with J. C. Adams he set about organizing a company, and in 1870 one was formed with a capital of $200,000. Previous to the organization of the company, Mr. Adams negotiated with the Newark Company, and the result was that the Cornell Company purchased the plant for $125,000, giving stock to that amount as payment.

Mr. Cornell set aside thirty acres of land as a site for the factory, erected a building at a cost of $75,000, taking stock in the company to that amount. The officers of the company were as follows: President, Paul Cornell; Vice President, C. M. Cady; Secretary, J. B. Jackson; Treasurer, Robert Schell; General Manager, T. C. Williams; General Agent, J. C. Adams.

In August, 1871, (just prior to the Chicago fire), the new building was completed and the machinery, etc., in the Newark factory brought on. The departments were as follows: Machine shop, plate room, train room, screw room, regulator and stud room, polishing room, wheel and pinion finishing room, stem-wind room, pinion and wheel room, 'scape wheel cutting room, jewel and pallet room, setting-up room, adjusting room, and dial room, fourteen in all. Owing to the frequent changes made in the heads of

THE CORNELL WATCH COMPANY'S FACTORY AT GRAND CROSSING, ILL.

the various departments it is almost impossible to give a list of the department superintendents with any degree of accuracy. The following gentlemen, however, may be named as having held various positions of trust during the career of this factory at Grand Crossing: Albert Troller, now superintendent of the Rockford Company; J. W. Hurd, late superintendent of the Aurora Company; John Penny, now with the Elgin Company; John Logan, now foreman of springing in Waltham factory; John Lucus, Chas. Boland, Frank Styles, E. Sandoz, C. L. Kidder, G. W. Hines, Thos. H. Wheeler, Geo. D. Clark, G. A. Kendrick, W. E. Piper, J. O. Newton, Isaac Holmes, Chas. Pegler, Alph. Jackson and C. R. Bacon. The latter gentleman acting as superintendent.

THE "GEO. F. ROOT" MOVEMENT.

The old movement made by the Newark Company was improved on, and new machinery and a great many new tools made. The company manufactured ten grades of movements, as follows: "Paul Cornell," "J. C. Adams," "Geo. F. Root," "John Evans," "H. N. Hibbard," "E. S. Williams," "C. T. Bowen," "C. M. Cady," "Geo. W. Waite," and "Ladies' Stem Wind." They were all 18-size, with the exception of the ladies' movement, and the greater majority were full plate and double sunk dial. Expansion balances were used. The "Paul Cornell" and "C. M. Cady" were stem-winders and the balance key-winders. The ladies' movement proved a failure, in spite of the fact that a trade paper in existence at the time said:

"One great feature of the Cornell Watch Company is, that they are the first in this county who have manufactured and introduced a 'Ladies' Stem Winding Watch,' which is, perhaps, in finish and originality of design, one of the greatest improvements of the age."

Mr. Cornell came to the conclusion that the Cornell Company was going to be a great success, and accordingly he began to purchase the stock as fast as possible, until, in about 1872, he found himself almost sole " monarch of all I survey." Two years after, however, he found the concern was not the successful one he had anticipated, and was ready to unload his stock. After corresponding with several parties he at length entered into negotiations with W. C. Ralston, a wealthy banker of San Francisco. In the fall of 1874 the entire plant was conveyed to the latter place, and such employes as could be induced to, were also taken to California.

Mr. Cornell's object in moving the factory was to take advantage of Chinese labor, which was then very cheap and plentiful in San Francisco. The new concern was called the Cornell Watch Company of San Francisco, with a capital of $250,000. The new company paid $100,000 for the Grand Crossing plant, which was then estimated as being worth $175,000. The officers were: President, W. C. Ralston; Vice-President, Oliver Eldridge; Secretary and Treasurer, James Cox.

An old building on Fourth street was remodeled as a factory. An effort was made to introduce Chinese labor, but the employes struck and raised so many obstacles in the way that the attempt was abandoned. In 1875 it was discovered that the company was in a critical position, and in the fall of that year Mr. Ralston, the President, committed suicide. January 1, 1876, the factory was closed. The California Watch Company succeeded the old company with a capital stock of $250,000. Berkely, a suburb of Oakland, was decided on as a site for the factory. A building was erected at the cost of $20,000. The old machinery was placed in the new factory, but operations were not resumed, as the company were undecided whether to start up with the old machinery or build new. They finally decided to wind up the business, as they saw no profit in starting up with the old tools, and were not in a condition to get new ones. They kept the machine shop running, however, until the summer of 1876, when the entire works were closed up.

Mr. Albert Troller, the present Superintendent of the Rockford factory, made arrangements with Messrs. Glickauf & Newhouse, then of San Francisco, to take the balance of the movements in the factory. In January, 1877, Mr. Troller bought all the unfinished material, leased the building, and proceeded to finish up all the movements. The movements were all finished early in the summer of 1877. The building and machinery were taken possession of by the Berkely Land Association, the machinery being eventually sold to the Independent Watch Company, of Fredonia, New York.

CHAPTER VI.

THE United States Watch Company was organized in July, 1864, with a capital stock of $500,000. The firm of Giles, Wales & Co., then wholesale dealers in watches and jewelry in New York City, were the organizers, and owned the controlling stock in the company. The officers of the company were F. A. Giles, President; William A. Wales, Secretary, Treasurer and General Business Manager. Directors: William A. Wales, G. C. F. Wright, F. A. Giles, S. M. Beard and A. H. Wallis.

Mr. James H. Gerry and several machinists from the Waltham factory were hired to build the machinery for the new factory. The company purchased a tract of land at Marion, N. J., and erected a building which was finished in 1865 at a cost of $125,000. It was constructed wholly of glass and iron in the proportion of five feet of glass to one foot of iron, and had a frontage of two hundred and fifty-three feet. The engine was an 80 horse power, and was built by the Putnam Machine Co., Fitchburg, Mass. An independent real-estate company was also formed, which was called the Marion Building Company. This company expended large amounts of money in laying out grounds and erecting buildings, hoping to reap a rich harvest when the factory got thoroughly under way. They were doomed to disappointment, however, as the site selected was not a very desirable one, and the land was easier to buy than to sell.

James H. Gerry was made superintendent; John Gardiner, foreman pinion finishing; Walter Farnsworth and Chas. Berlin, nickel finishing; William Sheppard, flat steel; Geo. Hart, plate room; E. S. Gerry, escapement room; Fred. Lowell, motion room; D. B. Gerry, stem-wind room; H. J. Cain, balance room; E. A. Hull, dial room, and William Smith, jewel room. Two hundred hands were employed.

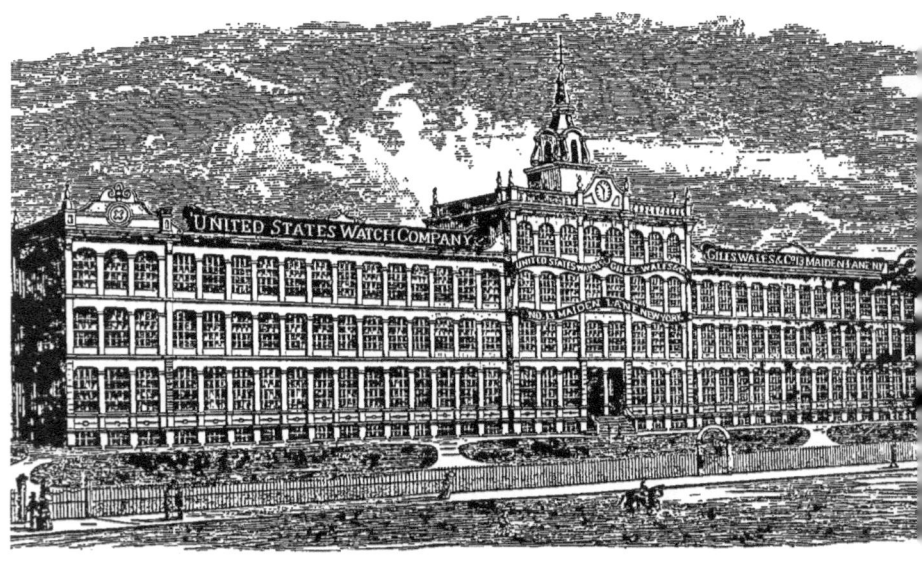

THE UNITED STATES WATCH COMPANY'S WATCH FACTORY, AT MARION, N. J.

The escapement was 18-size, straight-line, full plate, expansion balance, exposed pallet jewels, having a hole in the top plate so that the escapement might be examined without taking the plates apart. The finer grades had three pairs of conical pivots, cap jeweled, in gold settings and were adjusted to heat, cold and position. The first movements put on the market were called the "Frederick Atherton," and were completed in 1867, the output then being but 20 movements per day.

In 1868 the capital stock of the company was increased to $1,000,000, Messrs. Giles, Wales & Co. taking $200,000 more stock, making $475,000 worth of stock owned and controlled by this firm alone. In 1868 James H., D. B. and E. S. Gerry left the employ of the United States Watch Company to enter that of the New York Watch Company, of Springfield, Mass. James H. Gerry was succeeded as superintendent by Wm. H. Learned, under whose supervision the "Fayette Stratton," "Geo. Channing" and "Edwin Rollo" were turned out. These movements were all 18-size, the "Stratton" being full nickel, the "Channing" nickel top plate, and the "Rollo" was made in brass.

THE UNITED STATES WATCH.

In the summer of 1869, William H. Learned was succeeded by H. J. Lowe. Under Mr. Lowe's supervision the "United States," "S. M. Beard," "A. H. Wallace," "John Lewis," "Alexander," "Henry Randel," "G. A. Reed," "J. W. Deacon," "Chas. G. Knapp," and "Asa Fuller" were brought out. Nearly every movement made by this company was named after employes or stockholders. The "Stratton" was named after Mr. F. S. Giles, the "Randel" after Henry Randel, a stockholder and member of the diamond firm of Randel, Baremore & Billings, the "Rollo" after Edward R. Pratt, an employe of Giles, Wales & Co.; the "Wallace" after Mr. A. H. Wallace, a stockholder; the "Channing," after G. C. F. Wright, of Giles, Wales & Co.; the "Beard" after Mr. S. M. Beard, a stockholder; the "Alexander" after Mr. James A. Alexander, of the Ætna Insurance Co., a stockholder; the "Reed" after Mr. G. A. Reed, of Deep River, Conn., a stockholder. The "United States" was the finest movement made by this company, if not the finest then made in this country. It was 16-size, ¾-plate, compensation balance, and Breguet hair spring, gold train, 19 ruby jewels, and was adjusted for position, heat and cold, and isochronism. It was an elegant movement, and the company always pointed to it with pride. Messrs. Giles, Bro. & Co., then situated at 83 and 85 State St., Chicago, were western agents, and Messrs. Giles, Wales & Co., 13 Maiden Lane, general agents of the company.

Like all new concerns of the kind, the United States Watch Company sunk considerable money in its buildings, tools, patents and stock, to say nothing of the large sums absorbed in experimental processes. They gradually began to run short of money, and finally were compelled to make an assignment in 1872 to Wm. Muirhead, of Jersey City. The firm of Giles, Wales & Co., had great faith in the concern, and had invested over $700,000 in its stock. After the assignment the factory was run under the name of the "Marion Watch Company," for about two years, when the mortgages were foreclosed, and the plant disposed of to the various companies then formed and forming. Some of the machinery was purchased by the Fredonia Watch Company and the Auburndale Watch Company, other portions by the Fitchburg Watch Company.

CHAPTER VII.

IN the spring of 1864, Messrs. Ira G. Blake and P. S. Bartlett, both of whom were at that time connected with the Waltham Watch Company, paid a visit to Chicago. They became acquainted with J. C. Adams, then a watchmaker, and talked over the prospects for starting a watch factory in Chicago. Mr. Adams coincided with their views on the subject and interested several capitalists in the scheme. Messrs. Blake and Bartlett gave a glowing description of the Waltham Watch Company's business; they waxed eloquent, and at length convinced the capitalists that if Waltham could manufacture watches by machinery and supply the Western states, surely Chicago could make watches by machinery and supply the demand in the Eastern states.

On August 27, 1864, a company was incorporated under the name of "The National Watch Company of Chicago, Illinois," with a capital of $100,000. The incorporators were Philo Carpenter, Howard Z. Culver, Benjamin W. Raymond, Geo. M. Wheeler, Thomas S. Dickerson, Edward H. Williams and W. Robbins.

Messrs. Adams and Wheeler made a visit to the East and the following gentlemen contracted with the company for five years: Messrs. Otis Hoyt, P. S. Bartlett, Charles S. Moseley, Geo. Hunter, D. R. Hartwell, Chas. E. Mason, D. G. Currier and J. K. Bigelow. It was decided that the factory should be located at Elgin, and a tract of thirty-five acres of land was donated to the company for a factory site by the business men of that place. A three-story frame building, 35x60 feet was erected on the water power and work begun on the watch tools and machines. D. G. Currier, a Waltham expert, was hired, and together with Messrs. Moseley and Hunter, the work was started. April 25, 1865, the company was reorganized under a special charter with a capital of $500,000. The first officers of the company were: Benjamin W. Raymond, Chicago, President; Philo Carpenter, Chicago, Vice-President; Thomas S. Dickerson, Chicago, Treasurer, and Geo. M. Wheeler, Chicago, Secretary. The first board of directors consisted of Messrs. B. W. Raymond, Philo Carpenter, H. Z. Culver, T. S. Dickerson, J. T. Ryerson, G. M. Wheeler and B. F. Lawrence. In the spring of this year work was commenced on the permanent factory, which consisted of a three-story and basement, brick and stone building, 40x40 feet, with two wings 27½x100 and 27½x86 feet, respectively.

Jan. 1, 1866, the machinery department was transferred to the new building. June 1st of the same year the work of manufacturing watch materials was begun, but it was not until April 1, 1867, that the first movement was delivered from the factory. This movement was named B. W. Raymond, in honor of the president of the company. This movement was not, however, like the original model, but was an 18-size, key wind, full-plate, with quick train and straight line escapement arranged to set on the face- and was adjusted to temperature. It was a four hole, extra jeweled movement, and was a success from the very start.

During the summer of 1866 the factory began to assume a somewhat busy aspect. One department after another was organized in rapid succession. The first foremen of the respective departments, were as follows: General superintendent, Charles S. Moseley; machine shop, George Hunter; plate and screw, P. S. Bartlett; jeweling, Chas. H. Bagley; train, J. K. Bigelow, with Otis Hoyt as assistant; balance, Eben Hancock; escapement, C. E. Mason; finishing, D. G. Currier; dial, John Webb; adjusting, J. F. Gilson; gilding, James Fairchild; flat steel, William M. Goodridge.

The officers of the company were subsequently changed and in 1867 they were: B. W. Raymond, President; B. F. Lawrence, Vice-President; G. M. Wheeler, Secretary. Directors, B. W. Raymond, H. Z. Culver, B. F. Lawrence, H. H. Taylor, G. M. Wheeler, J. T. Ryerson and T. M. Avery.

On July 16, 1867, a new watch was turned out which was named the H. Z. Culver. The slow train was then adopted on all the new movements brought out and they appeared on the market as follows: J. T. Ryerson, Oct. 14, 1867; H. H. Taylor, Nov. 20, 1867; G. M. Wheeler, Nov. 26, 1867; Matthew Laflin, Jan. 4, 1868.

Otis Hoyt left his home in Amesbury to go to work for the Waltham company in 1858. He severed his connection with the company at the time of the war, and served as captain until he was honorably discharged in July, 1864. In the fall of that year he joined forces with Geo. Hunter and several others and went to Elgin, contracting with that company for a term or five years. His health failed him, however, and in 1867 he was compelled to go to California for a change of climate, and from there he returned to Waltham. He soon went to Springfield, Ill., to act as superintendent, and remained in that position until 1871, when he went to Elgin to take charge of the train room, a position which he filled creditably for fourteen years. He died at his residence in Elgin, June 2, 1885, in his forty-eighth year.

Mr. Benjamin W. Raymond, who was made president of the company after its organization, served until Oct. 10, 1867, when he was succeeded by T. M. Avery, who has since held the office. Mr. G. M. Wheeler, the secretary, was succeeded by Mr. Hiram Reynolds in January, 1868.

January 28, 1869, the authorized capital of the company was increased to $2,000,000.

May 20, 1869, the "Lady Elgin" made its appearance on the market. It was the first of the series of 10-size key wind, ladies' movements, and proved very popular. It was followed by the Francis Rubie, which was adjusted to temperature, appearing August 24, 1870; the Gail Borden, September 8, 1871, and the Dexter Street, December 20, 1871.

Mr. Benj. F. Lawrence, the vice-president of the company, died December 16, 1871, and Mr. Geo. N. Culver was elected to fill the vacant chair.

On June 28, 1873, the first stem-wind movement was placed on the market. It was a Raymond movement made over, and was shortly followed by the Culver, Taylor, Wheeler, Laflin and Ogden.

THE "B. W. RAYMOND" MOVEMENT.

At a special meeting of the stockholders of the company held in Chicago, May 12, 1874, it was decided to change the name of the company to "The Elgin National Watch Company." This was thought to be advisable because the movements manufactured by the company were universally known as and called "Elgin Watches." In March, 1875, the company began to make its own mainsprings, which had prior to that time been purchased ready made. June

THE FACTORY OF THE ELGIN NATIONAL WATCH COMPANY, AT ELGIN, ILL.

16, 1875, the first watches called by the name of the company, were placed on the market, and were designated by numbers.

Seven new grades of 10 size, six grades of 12 size and five grades of 14 size, three-quarter plate, key wind movements, were made by the company between Sept. 29, 1875, and Dec. 29, 1876. Most of these new patterns were made for the foreign markets, which demanded movements differing in some respects from those made for home consumption. So large was the demand for Elgin movements during the year 1876, that the factory, although running over time, and turning out movements as fast as the capacity would admit of, yet the orders were far behind, and dealers were beginning to complain. The London office of the company was closed, the forces increased, and everything possible was done to meet the enormous demand.

In January, 1877, Mr. Hiram Reynolds, the Secretary, was succeeded by Mr. George R. Noyes.

The company placed its first nickel movement upon the market, August 15, 1877.

A new line of 8 size, stem wind movements were placed upon the market, June 11, 1878. In the fall of 1878 four grades of 16 size, three-quarter plate, stem-wind movements were brought out. These movements were interchangeable, in hunting and open face cases, and were at that time considered quite a novelty.

Mr. George R. Noyes died in July, 1879, leaving vacant the office of secretary, and Mr. Whitehead was elected and served until June, 1884, when he was succeeded by Mr. William G. Prall.

Henry H. Taylor died November 9, 1875; William H. Ferry, died March 26, 1880; J. T. Ryerson died March 9, 1883; Benjamin W. Raymond died April 5, 1883.

Mr. George N. Culver filled the position of Vice-President until June, 1884, when Mr. James W. Scoville was elected to that position.

Upon the death of Otis Hoyt, foreman of the train room, in June, 1885, his assistant, Mr. George E. Farrington, was promoted to the position of foreman.

For a number of years the mainsprings were made by Prenot of Philadelphia, but later on the company made their own springs. The "Burt patent" to prevent accident in case of mainspring breakage was the invention of Mr. Merritt Burt of Cleveland, Ohio, and modified by Mr. Chas. S. Moseley.

The factory is producing at present about 7,500 movements per week, about one-fifth of which are key wind and one-tenth nickel. About 2,300 persons are employed. The various positions are at present occupied as follows : President, T. M. Avery; Vice-President, J. W. Scoville; Secretary, William G. Prall; Directors, T. M. Avery, J. W. Scoville, George H. Laflin, Chas. Fargo, Martin Ryerson, G. N. Culver and M. C. Town; General Agents, J. M. Cutter, Chicago; C. J. Scofield, New York; Superintendent, Geo. Hunter; Asst. Supt., William H. Cloudman; Cashier, Carlos H. Smith; Book-keeper, W. P. Hemmens; Shipping Clerk, J. McLaughlin; Material Clerk, H. L. Given; foreman finishing department A, William H. Black: finishing B, J. H. Moulton; motion, F. H. Corthell; escapement, George E. Hunter; stem-wind, William C. Torrey; screw, Frank Preston; gilding, William Hewins; engraving, A. F. Kelsey; jeweling, L. N. Jackson; dial, F. B. Perkins; balance, E. F. Gooding; train, G. E. Farrington; plate, Hiram Thomas; flat steel, A. F. Alden; mainspring, Charles Lehman; hand and press, C. L. Young; machine, W. F. Dean; timing, Ira Pixley; master watchmaker, C. P. Corliss; mechanical engineer, Frank Leman; superintendent gas, water and steam, A. L. Harrington; head carpenter, D. R. Hartwell.

The floor area of the present building is 169,000 square feet, not including the detached buildings, such as the gas house, 52 x 180 feet, the purifying house, 30x64 feet, the generating house, 60x118 feet, carpenter shop, 30 x 135 feet, and engine house. From the above it will be seen that the company makes all its own gas, which is of a superior quality. The water is furnished by an artesian well, and all known precautions against fire have been taken. The factory has its own steam fire engine, a trained fire brigade, one hundred dozen fire grenades, and a Holly system of water works, with a capacity of eight one inch streams. Two eighty horse power engines provide the power for this mammoth institution.

J. C. ADAMS.

CHAPTER VIII.

AS a watch factory organizer Mr. J. C. Adams has probably had more experience than any living man, and his name is familiar to every watchmaker and jeweler in this country. Mr. Adams was born in Preble, N. Y., October 7, 1834. His father was a prosperous farmer. When he was but two years of age his father sold his farm and removed to Syracuse, N. Y. In 1842 he gathered together his chattles and removed to what was then termed the far west, locating in Elgin, Ill. Mr. Adams served a five years' apprenticeship to John H. Atkins, an old Liverpool watchmaker. After finishing his apprenticeship he was engaged as watchmaker by S. C. Spalding, of Janesville, Wis. After two years employment by Mr. Spalding, he again returned to Elgin and entered into partnership with G. B. Adams, the firm being known as G. B. & J. C. Adams. At the end of two years the partnership was dissolved and Mr. Adams went to Chicago and was employed in the watch department of Messrs. Hoard & Hoes. In 1861 he managed the watch department of W. H. & C. Miller, Chicago, and had an interest in that department. In 1862 he was appointed time keeper for the various railroads centering in Chicago.

In the spring of 1864, Mr. Adams severed his connection with W. H. & C. Miller and together with Messrs. Chas. S. Moseley and P. S. Bartlett, organized the Elgin Watch Company. In 1869, together with Mr. Paul Cornell, he organized the Cornell Watch Company of

Grand Crossing, Ill., and served for some time as general agent of that company. One of the movements made by this company was named in his honor.

In 1869, Mr. Adams, together with Springfield capitalists, organized the Illinois Watch Company at Springfield.

In 1874 he organized the Adams & Perry Watch Manufacturing Company, and became Secretary and General Manager of the company. He resigned his position in the fall of 1875.

In 1883 he entered the employ of the Independent Watch Company of Fredonia, N. Y. In 1885 he organized the Peoria Watch Company and continued with that company until April 14, 1888. He is the inventor and patentee of " The Adams System of Time Records " which is employed on nearly every western railroad.

CHAPTER IX.

AARON L. DENNISON, as previously described, was not discouraged by his somewhat checkered experience as an organizer and stockholder of watch companies, but made a final effort to right himself. In 1864 he visited A. O. Bigelow, of Boston, and explained his ideas to him in regard to the establishment of a factory on a somewhat novel basis. At that time there was a good demand for a medium-priced movement, and the field was far from being occupied. After some deliberation the Tremont Watch Company, was organized in April, 1864, with a capital stock of $100,000. Mr. Dennison's idea was to have certain parts of the movements made in Switzerland, where labor was cheap, shipped to the United States, and with the other parts, which were to be made in America, set up and adjusted. By doing this, he argued, the company could put their product on the market in a much shorter space of time, and could save the expense of building complicated and expensive machinery, and a large building.

Mr. Dennison was elected superintendent of the company, and was to go to Switzerland to see to the manufacture of the parts that were thought best to have manufactured there. The plates, barrels and some minor parts were to be made in Boston, and after getting together the necessary machinery, the work was started. D. B. Bingham was made superintendent of the Boston shop, with Charles P. Crafts as foreman. D. F. Leary had charge of the jeweling; John Polsey, plate room; Andrew Brush, gilding;

O. Jenkins, master watchmaker, and C. Byam was foreman of the flat steel work.

Mr. Dennison went to Zurich, where he hired a shop, and commenced work on the trains, balances and escapements. Most of the work was done outside the shop, and Mr. Denison contracted with various parties to furnish certain portions of the work. Several competent men were employed to work in the shop where the balances were tried, the escapements matched, and the pivoting done. The first movements, which were 18-size, full jeweled, were placed on the market in the summer of 1865.

In 1866 the company decided to move the factory to Melrose, Mass., and manufacture the entire movement in this country. Mr. Dennison was strongly opposed to this change as the company were doing a very good business, and the outlook was very encouraging. He prophesied that if the change was made the company would surely come to grief. The officers of the company, however, had decided on the change, and accordingly a frame building 50 x 100 feet was purchased, and the old tools and machinery moved in, and arrangements made for the manufacture of new ones. Mr. Dennison then withdrew from the company as a stockholder, but continued to furnish the company with material until the new tools were well under way. The old movement was remodeled and engraved "Melrose Watch Company." About this time the company began to run short of funds, and called upon the stockholders for the additional fifty per cent. of the capital stock. The stockholders, however, failed to come to time, and in 1868 Mr. Dennison's prophesy came true. Mr. Dennison was asked to sell the plant in Switzerland, but could find no purchasers. In 1870 Mr. Dennison returned to Boston, and tried to organize a new company, and buy the old plant. Failing in this, he went to England, where he effected a sale of the machinery to what is now known as the "English Watch Company."

CHAPTER X.

THE Mozart Watch Company was organized in the spring of 1864, the incorporators being mostly wholesale and manufacturing jewelers of New York City and Providence. The office and factory of the company was located in Providence, R.I. The capital stock was $100,000.

The watch which the company proposed to manufacture was 18-size; and was known as the "three-wheeled Mozart," the invention of D. J. Mozart, of Xenia, Ohio. Geo. S. Rice was President; J. A. Briggs, Secretary, and Mr. Mozart was made Superintendent. Work was immediately commenced on the machinery and tools, and in the fall of 1864 work was commenced upon the movement, and then the trouble began to brew. The stockholders finally decided that the Mozart watch would never be a success, and that the sooner they abandoned it the better off they would be. This was in the spring of 1866, and in the summer of the same year L. W. Cushing, of Waltham, was placed in Mr. Mozart's position, with instructions to build the necessary machinery for the manufacture of a regular 18-size three-quarter plate lever movement. The name of the company was then changed to "The New York Watch Company." In 1867 the company purchased two buildings, and a piece of ground in Springfield, Mass., and moved the machinery there. The buildings consisted of a large boarding house, and a large building which had previously been occupied as a machine shop. After moving to Springfield the company was reorganized and the capital increased to $300,000. The former president and secretary retained their offices, and George Walker was elected as Treasurer, and O. P. Rice became business manager. In 1868 James H. Gerry, who was in the employ of the United States Watch Company, was secured and placed in the position of superintendent. The factory was destroyed by fire April 25, 1870, but many of the machines and part of the material was saved. The company then cleared away the debris, and moved the boarding house into the position previously occupied by the

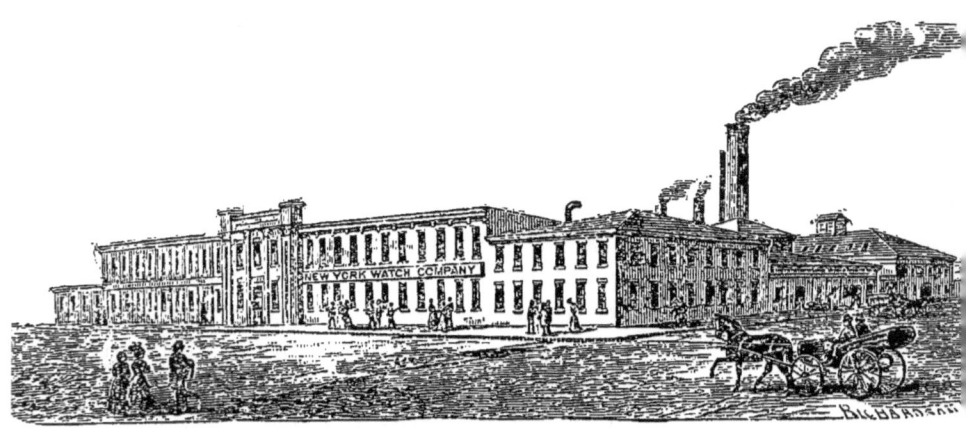

NEW YORK WATCH COMPANY'S FACTORY, AT SPRINGFIELD, MASS., DESTROYED BY FIRE APRIL,

factory. It was remodeled, and in about three months the factory was in operation again. The first movements placed on the market were 18-size, three-quarter plate, lever movements, with straight line escapement. These movements were known as "Springfield," "John L. King," "Homer Foot," "No. 5," "J. A. Briggs," "H. G. Norton," and "Albert Clark." In 1871 the company placed an 18-size full plate movement on the market.

The factory did well until the year of the great panic, 1873, when they began to fall behind. They finally pulled through 1873 and 1874 by reducing the number of employ-

ces, but in 1875 they decided to close the factory. The stockholders reorganized under the name of the New York Watch Manufacturing Company. This did not last long, however, for in about eight months the factory was again closed. In 1877 the stock and bond holders reorganized under a new title with fresh capital, having purchased the machinery of the old company. Of the new company, which was known as the Hampden Watch Company, we will speak in another chapter.

Mr. James H. Gerry, who was made superintendent in 1868, retired early in 1870, and was succeeded by Mr. Osmore Jenkins, who was in turn succeeded by Mr. H. J. Cain. D. B. Gerry, E. S. Gerry, Geo. Hunt, Geo. Griffin, Chas. P. Crafts, Charles Ayer, Leo Murray and George Pollard held various positions in the factory in its younger days. The various movements were the "Frederick Billings," a full jeweled, 18-size, adjusted movement; the "George Walker," an 18-size, three-quarter plate; the "New York Watch Company," a 16-size three-quarter plate; the "John Hancock," a cheap 18-size, seven jewel, key wind; the "Geo. Sance Rice," an 18-size, seven jewel, imitation expansion balance, and the "Chas. E. Hayward," an 18-size, eleven jewel, imitation expansion balance.

THE NEW YORK WATCH.

CHAPTER XI.

SOON after his discharge by the Providence company, in 1866, as described in a previous chapter, D. J. Mozart moved to Ann Arbor, Michigan, where he proceeded to organize a company known as the "Mozart Watch Company." The capital stock was two hundred thousand dollars, and the incorporators were W. A. Benedict, Don J. Mozart, C. T. Wilmot, W. W. Wheedon, A. J. Southerland and Charles Tripp. The officers of the company were, Prest. Chas. Tripp; Treasurer, W. W. Wheedon, and Secretary, A. J. Southerland. Mr. Mozart was made Superintendent. A factory was rented, and machinists hired to build the necessary machinery. The movement was the same as that which he tried to have the Mozart Company, of Providence, introduce, and was seventeen size. Obstacles of various kinds began to present themselves, and the progress of the work did not please the stockholders. Nearly three years had elapsed since the organization of the company and there was no fruits to show for the labor and money expended. The money began to run short, and in the winter of 1870

THE "THREE-WHEELED" MOZART.

the stockholders decided to sell out if a buyer could be found. Some thirty odd movements were finished at this time, all of them given to stockholders and friends, and none being placed on the market.

A company was organized in Rock Island, Illinois, and after an inspection of the machinery, decided to purchase it. The price paid for the plant was $40,000 : $25,000 in stock of the new company, and a note for the balance. No available site could be found for the factory at Rock Island, and accordingly the town of Milan, some seven miles below the city, was selected as a fitting place for the factory. The officers of the company were, J. A. Wilson, President; C. M. Aiken, Secretary and Business Manager. Frank Leman, now designer for the Elgin Company, was engaged as Superintendent. G. B. McElwain, of Chicago, made the model watch for the Company, which was somewhat like the Mozart movement. After the machinery was moved to Milan, and placed on the floor of the new building, the stockholders came to the conclusion that it was not just what they wanted, and refused to pay the notes for $15,000. The Mozart Company sent a representative to Milan to arbitrate their claim, which resulted in the return of the machinery to the Mozart Company and the payment of $5,000.

FREEPORT MOVEMENT.

In 1874 a stock company was formed at Freeport, Illinois, with a capital of $250,000. The incorporators and officers of this company were residents of Ann Arbor, Michigan, and Freeport, Illinois. Part of the old Mozart plant was purchased for $51,000; $1,000 cash and $50,000 in stock in the new company. A brick building was erected in Freeport, 40x100 feet and the machinery moved into it. This company never manufactured many movements, however, as the factory was burned down on the night of October 21, 1875, and the building and contents were a total loss. The company were insured for $30,000.

CHAPTER XII.

THE Illinois Springfield Watch Company was organized in January, 1869, with a capital stock of $100,000, with T. J. Stuart as President, W. B. Miller, Secretary, and a Board of Directors, consisting of John W. Bunn, Geo. Passfield, John Williams, Geo. Black and the Secretary and President. The company was organized mainly through the efforts of J. C. Adams. Mr. Adams employed a number of experienced men in Elgin to build the machinery for the new company, and work was commenced on the building. This was in the spring of 1870, and the building was ready for occupancy in the fall of the same year. The first watch was turned out early in 1872. In 1873 a New York office was opened, with J. M. Morrow as agent, and in 1879 a Chicago office was opened, with L. W. Arnold as manager, a position which he occupied until early in 1887. The hard times of 1873 and 1874 placed the company in an embarassing position. They had a large surplus of finished movements on hand and little or no demand existed. They pulled through however, after a desperate effort, but were short of ready funds. In 1875 a new company was organized, that assumed all the liabilities of the old one. The capital stock of this company was placed at $250,000 and E. N. Bates elected President. The new company however, met with no better success than the old one, and although the working force was enlarged and the product considerably increased, yet the company steadily lost money. In 1879 the company was again reorganized and Jacob Bunn, one of the original stockholders, elected President. The name of the company was changed to the Springfield Illinois Watch Company. The early product of the factory was known as the "Hoyt," "Stuart," "Mason," "Bunn" and "Miller." The first stem-wind movement was made in 1875 and the first ladies' movement in 1876. In the early part of 1886 the company put upon the market their four-size ladies' watch, which at that time was the smallest watch made in the United States.

The following gentlemen have served in the capacity of foremen of different departments at various times; Otis Hoyt, C. E. Mason, D. G. Currier, W. F. Dean, J. K. Biglow, John Wilkenson, John Leman, Eben Hancock, John Pegler, and Ferd. F. Ide. The first superintendent was J. K. Biglow, who served in that capacity from April, 1870 until July, 1873, when

THE ILLINOIS MOVEMENT.

he was succeeded by D. G. Currier, who served until 1875, when he was in turn succeeded by Otis Hoyt. Mr. Hoyt was succeeded in March, 1878 by C. E. Mason. The plant of the Company is located upon fourteen acres of ground just outside the city limits of Springfield, on North Grand Avenue between Ninth and Eleventh Streets. The buildings are of brick, with stone trimmings, and the visitor is at once impressed with their compact and at the same time convenient arrangement. The main factory building has a frontage of 250 feet, and consists of a central building, 40x50 feet, and four stories in height and two wings, each 30x100 feet, three stories in height.

FACTORY OF THE ILLINOIS WATCH COMPANY, AT SPRINGFIELD, ILL.

There are two wings, three stories high, which branch from the large main wings, besides a gas house, annex and several small buildings.

At present the company employ 900 hands and turn out about 400 finished movements daily. The present officers of the company are Jacob Bunn, President; John W. Bunn, Vice President; Geo. A. Bates, Acting Secretary; A. E. Bently, Manager. The present Board of Directors consists of Jacob Bunn, J. W. Bunn, B. H. Ferguson, Geo. A. Bates, Thos. C. Henkle, and Henry Bunn.

Mr. F. W. Cory is the manager of the New York office and G. G. Gubbins, manager of Chicago office.

The seventeen departments of the factory are presided over as follows: Machine, Eugine E. Bradford; plate, C. A. Bradeen; gilding, Wm. Palmer; hand punch, D. Nash Mitchell; mainspring, John Lehmann; flat steel and screw, J. D. Lowe; pinion roughing, D. W. Chalmers; pinion cutting, J. H. Burns; pinion finishing, C. G. Village; balance, A. H. Smith; jeweling, A. H. Ranzenberger; motion, S. J. Caughey; stem wind, N. M. Benson; escapement, J. F. Crowe; dial. C. B. Nichols; timing, T. Presternd; finishing A, W. J. Evans; finishing C, J. Pedersen.

CHAPTER XIII.

THE Rockford Watch Company was organized in March 1874, with a capital stock of $150,000. The incorporators were H. P. Holland, Israel Sovereign and George Troxell. The company immediately proceeded to construct the necessary tools and machinery and build a suitable factory. The factory was completed early in 1876, and the necessary tools and machinery moved into it. The first officers of the company were: President, Levi Rhodes, Vice Prest., Henry W. Price; Treasurer, George Troxell. The first Board of Directors consisted of George D. Clarke, Orlando Clarke, A. D. Forbes, Thos. Butterworth, Israel Sovereign, S. P. Crawford and the President, Vice Prest. and Treasurer. The company placed its first goods upon the market in the fall of 1876. Most of the employes came from the Cornell Watch Company's factory at Grand Crossing. Geo. D. Clarke was made Superintendent and P. H. Wheeler assistant Superintendent. Mr. Clarke was succeeded in 1876 by J. W. Hurd. The foremen were as follows: U. C. Osborne, polishing; J. E. Tobin, springing; J. D. Camp, pinions; C. W. Parker, plate room, and G. A. Hines, jeweling.

After due consideration, the company decided that they would sell their products direct to the retail trade, and were the pioneers of this system. They also decided that it was better to make a small number of watches of a good quality, rather than a large number of indifferent quality. The company soon found that there was a steadily increasing demand for a watch suitable for railroad men, and they decided to make all their movements quick train.

The Rockford Company, unlike many others of its kind, met with success from the start, and has never been compelled to close its doors. Much of this success is due to excellent judgment and rare business ability and foresight of its managers, but not a little is also due to the excellency of its products.

The factory, which is situated in a commanding position upon a bluff, is a three story brick and stone structure, occupying a frontage of 96 feet, and consists of a central building 32 x 125 feet with two wings, each 32 x 70 feet. The present product of the company is 150 movements per day, and 350 persons are employed.

The fourteen different departments of the factory are presided over as follows:

Superintendent, Albert Troller. Foreman machine and die, John A. Johnson ; plate, John Glynn ; gilding, Thomas Conway; escape and flat steel, J. S. Clark; screw, Bert Waters; springing, timing and adjusting, James E. Tobin; pinion roughing, Fred Lake; pinion finishing, Louis C. Grassell; balance, Fred Gork; jeweling, Guy H. Cutting; motion, W. H. Colburn; dial, E. J. Guilford; polishing, U. C. Osborne; matching, William Wildt; finishing, James C. Gaskins.

The officers of the company are: President, Henry W. Price; Secretary, Hosmer P. Holland; Treasurer, J. P. Drake.

CHAPTER XIV.

IN May, 1874, several prominent citizens of Lancaster, Pa., together with J. C. Adams, organized a watch company with a capital stock of $78,000. In June of the same year a Board of Directors was elected together with the following officers: President, E. J. Zahm; Vice-President, John Best; Sec'y and Gen'l Manager, J. C. Adams, and Treasurer, J. B. Roath. The company was incorporated Sept. 26, 1874, under the name of the Adams & Perry Watch Mfg. Co. E. H. Perry was appointed superintendent and several of his patents were adopted by the company, a royalty of three dollars per movement being paid to him. A machine shop was started and work on the tools and machinery commenced.

Mr. C. A. Bitner, of Lancaster, donated a three-acre tract of land as a site for a factory and work on the building was commenced in the fall of 1874. The factory was completed in the summer of 1875, and the tools and machinery were moved in. About this time the first misunderstanding arose. Mr. Adams' plan was to import the escapements, etc., but his suggestions were overruled and those of Mr. Perry, to manufacture the complete movement in the factory, were adopted. Mr. Adams thereupon resigned his position both as Secretary and Manager.

In the fall of 1875 the company found themselves pressed for ready funds and accordingly bonds to the amount of $25,000 were issued. The first movement was finished April, 7, 1876, twenty-two months after starting the building of the machinery. The great delay in getting out the movements involved considerable expense and the company again found themselves in an embarrassing position. An effort was made to increase the capital stock, but it proved a failure, and the factory was closed May 16, 1876.

Efforts were immediately set on foot and a new company was organized. The old directors then resigned and were succeeded by eleven new ones. The following resolutions were then adopted: "That all contracts with operatives be annulled. That all the patents owned by E. H. Perry shall be assigned to the company, with the proviso that if Mr. Perry shall leave the company he shall have the right to allow one other company to use them. That the royalty hereafter be paid to Mr. Perry be $1 for each movement. That the directors raise $50,000 by issuing covertible mortgage bonds, or by any other means, and that said bonds be sold to the stockholders at 80 per cent of their face, and any part of said bonds remaining unsold to be placed upon the market at par. That the capital stock be increased to $250,000 and Mr. A. Bitner appointed manager."

THE KEYSTONE MOVEMENT.

The following officers were then elected: President, Dr. H. Carpenter; Vice-President, B. F. Eshelman; Treasurer, C. A. Bitner; Sec'y, J. P. McCasky; Manager, Abraham Bitner. For some unknown reason the bonds above mentioned were never issued, and on June 10, 1876, the company being pushed by their creditors were obliged to make an assignment to C. A. Bitner, who sold the property at public sale. It was purchased by Dr. Carpenter for a syndicate for $47,000, subject to two mortgages aggregating $30,000.

In August, 1877, the Lancaster Watch Company was formed, and they advanced a cash capital of $21,000, consisting of seven shares of $3,000 each. These shares were

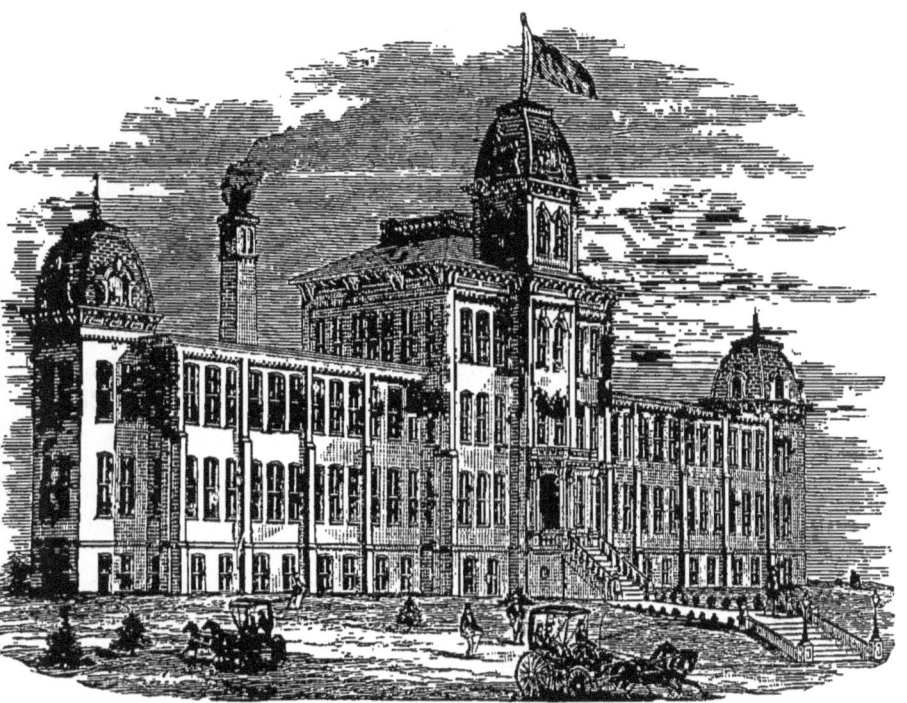

THE FACTORY OF THE KEYSTONE WATCH COMPANY, LANCASTER, PA.

owned by A. Bitner, S. F. Rathfou, John Best, Bitner & Hostetter, Eshelman & Rathfou, J. P. McCasky, and H. S. Gurra. Work was commenced Sept. 1, 1877, and a new movement was designed and modeled. It was a three-quarter plate, full jeweled. In the fall of 1878 the capital stock was increased $35,000, mainly through the efforts of Mr. A. Bitner.

The company was reorganized Oct. 31, 1878, under the name of the Lancaster, Pa., Watch Company, Limited, with a capital of $160,000. The old model adopted by the company not proving satisfactory, a new one was ordered, but before any of this pattern could be placed upon the market the company again found itself short of ready funds. An attempt was made to borrow money, but owing to a misunderstanding among the stockholders, this proved a failure. A new company was formed May 9, 1879, under the title of the Lancaster Watch Company. The new company leased the property, paying 6 per cent. interest, taxes and insurance; this lease was for a term not to exceed five years, the interest being based on a valuation of $130,000. The following officers were then elected: Prest., J. I. Hartmann; Sec'y., J. P. McCasky; Treas., J. D. Skyles. Mr. A. Bitner was appointed Manager. Things went on swimmingly for some time, the product being greatly increased, and in April, 1883, the Lancaster Watch Company surrendered its lease to the owners, the Lancaster, Pa., Watch Company. The two companies then consolidated with a capital stock of $248,000, with the same officers and a few slight changes in the board of directors. In July, 1883, the factory was again closed, but later on the board succeeded in borrowing $25,000 and work was resumed, although a heavy indebtedness had accumulated and many of the stockholders began to grow uneasy. Mr. Bitner then made the dissatisfied stockholders a proposition to take their stock off their hands without compensation and assume all indebtedness. Several large stockholders transferred their stock and together with other blocks which he purchased at ridiculously low figures, Mr. Bitner soon became the owner of 5,625 of the 8,000 shares.

In 1886 the Keystone Standard Watch Co., with a full paid capital of $500,000 purchased the factory. Its officers are: President, Dr. C. M. Shellenberger; Vice-President, Geo. M. Franklin; Sec'y and Treas., W. Z. Sener. Directors, Geo. M. Franklin and W. Z. Sener, of Lancaster, and Dr. C. M. Shellenberger, Stanton Wilgus and W. J. Atkinson, of Philadelphia.

The officers of the new company are all men of means, ability and energy, with the reputation of having succeeded in every enterprise they have ever undertaken. Under their control the factory has been steadily increasing its output and the quality of its goods. They expect within a short time to reach a production of at least 300 a day.

The superintendents and foremen are as follows: Superintendent, Abraham Bitner; ass't supt., J. H. Koch; master mechanic, W. H. Denny; foreman, train, Joseph Buettner; plate, Wesley Rooney; screw, A. Burkhart; jeweling, A. Buch; motion, Joel Baker; balance, C. E. Wilson; flat steel, W. Coho; escape, H. Coho; springing, Marcus Keeport; finishing, E. Snyder; gilding, Joseph Gorde; dial making, Frank Rooney; dial painting, George Hetrick; inspector John W. Bitner.

Their entire product is placed through Atkinson Bros., of Philadelphia, who sell mainly to the jobbing trade.

CHAPTER XV.

IN the year 1875, Mr. S. Sawyer of Fitchburg, Mass., concluded to start a watch factory in the town in which he resided. His idea was to build the necessary machinery, make a model movement and when everything was ready, to interest capital and organize a watch company. Accordingly he entered into negotiations with Mr. H. J. Lowe, who had previously been a superintendent in the United States watch factory, and after renting a suitable building the manufacture of the necessary machinery was commenced. Several gentlemen, who were formerly connected with the United States Watch Company, were engaged to see to the building of the machinery, among them being Messrs. Thos. Parker, A. R. Bardeen, Chas. Whitehouse and Gilbert Crowell. Mr. Crowell was made superintendent and the work went on at a very lively rate.

At the end of three years the machinery was well under way and Mr. Sawyer went in search of capitalists who were willing to invest their money in a watch factory. Previous to this time Mr. Lowe severed his connection with the concern owing to his ill-health. Mr. Sawyer's search was not rewarded with success and his own money having given out he decided to cease operations until moneyed parties could be found. Work was accordingly stopped, the employes discharged and the factory was closed up. Subsequently Mr. Crowell returned to Fitchburg and was associated with Mr. Sawyer in the Sawyer Watch Tool Co. Part of the old machinery was used in their business and the balance was sold to Cornell and other watch companies. At the time of closing the factory, the necessary machinery for an output of twenty-five movements per day was finished. The machinery cost Mr. Sawyer $45,000 exclusive of rent and taxes and he realized very little of this amount from the sales.

CHAPTER XVI.

IN 1876, J. R. Hopkins, together with W. A. Wales, visited Auburndale, Mass., with a view to interesting W. B. Fowle, a capitalist of that place, in a watch factory project. The movement which they proposed to manufacture was known as the " rotary," and was invented by Mr. Hopkins. It was somewhat similar in construction to the Waterbury and like it, it made a complete revolution once every hour. It was an 18-size, anchor escapement, and was stem wind and set. Mr. Fowle, after an investigation, concluded there was money in the project and soon after made arrangements for the erection of a factory. Negotiations were entered into with Geo. E. Hart, of Newark, N. J., for the manufacture of the machinery. This machinery required considerable overhauling and remodeling, nevertheless, the first movements were finished in the fall of 1877 and were immediately placed upon the market. They were cased in open faced nickel cases and sold at ten dollars each to the trade. Very soon complaints began to come to the manufacturers that these movements were defective and the greater majority of them were taken back by the firm. In all, about one thousand movements were made and the greater majority of them found their way into the waste heap. The Auburndale Rotary was not a success, but the management were not discouraged and immediately began work on a new movement invented by Mr. Hopkins, and known as the Auburndale Timer. They were 18-size, $\frac{1}{4}$, $\frac{1}{8}$ and 1-10 seconds. The " Timer " was improved by A. Craig, J. H. Gerry and W. A. Wales. Mr. Craig, who was master mechanic, invented the stop and starting arrangement and Mr. Gerry invented the escapement. At this time the management of the factory was as follows:

W. E. Rae, the first superintendent, died very suddenly of heart disease and his position was filled by Wm. Geust, who was in turn succeeded by J. H. Gerry, who was succeeded in 1878 by G. H. Bourne, who was succeeded by E. H. Perry, who was succeeded by J. Hinds, who was succeeded by O. L. Strout. B. F. Gerry was foreman escapement making; Thomas Steele, foreman train room; Fredk. H. Eaves, foreman motion and jeweling rooms; John Rowe, foreman flat steel; A. Craig, master mechanic; W. Simmons, plate, and O. L. Strout, springing and finishing room. The general management of the business was in the hands of Messrs. Wales and Fowle.

THE AUBURNDALE ROTARY.

In 1878 Chauncey Hartwell, under the direction of the management, made a model of an 18-size, three-quarter plate movement, and work was immediately commenced on these watches. Mr. Hartwell was a practical watchmaker having had many years experience in the Waltham factory. The first of these movements made their appearance in the summer of 1879, the " Bently " was a stem-wind and the " Lincoln " a key-wind, and both were gilt movements. About three hundred of these movements were manufactured when the idea was abandoned, as the movements could not be sold at a price that would realize any profit for the manufacturers. The manufacture of these movements was started at a very dull time, when all watches were a drug on the market, and the company tried to make a three-quarter plate to compete in price with the cheap full plate, that the others companies were then making. At the time they were the only cheap three-quarter plate movements on the market and were very well made, considering the very poor facilities they then had for making them. Probably in the history of modern watch-making, no company had so may difficulties to overcome and showed such good results from their labors.

In 1879 a stock company was formed of which Mr. Fowle was made President and G. H. Bourne, Secretary and Treasurer. After abandoning the "Bentley" and "Lincoln" movements the company turned their attention to the manufacture of dial thermometers and horse-timers. They continued in this business until 1881, when they abandoned the timers and devoted their entire attention to thermometers.

The "Timer" was, as far as the manufacture was concerned, a success, but a want of business push and enterprize on the part of the management was lacking and consequently, although the goods were acknowledged to be of a fair quality, yet sales were very slow.

The company failed in the fall of 1883, and early in the following year the machinery was sold. Those who are in a position to judge are confident that the original Auburndale Rotary would have been a success had the proper machinery been made for its manufacture and a few changes made in its construction. It was a simple movement and was therefore inexpensive to manufacture.

CHAPTER XVII.

THE Hampden Watch Company was organized in January, 1877, virtually succeeding the New York Watch Manufacturing Company as described in Chapter X. Homer Foote was the first President, and Chas. D. Rood, Treasurer and Business Manager. The first Board of Directors was composed of Homer Foote, Jas. D. Baur, A. Breever and Aaron Bragg. H. J. Cain was made superintendent and still occupies that position. The old movement of the New York Company was remodeled, and the factory opened in the summer of 1877. In 1881 a new brick building was erected, 40 x 100 feet, and three stories and basement. Five buildings were then used by the company, the main one being 30 x 120 feet, brick, three stories and basement, and has a central tower. The other buildings are respectively 33 x 50, 40 x 100, 45 x 90 and 40 x 80. The company turn out fourteen grades of movements, which are all full-plate, with the exception of the " State Street," which is 16-size, three-quarter plate and gilded steel. The power is furnished by a ninety-horse power engine, situated in a building back of the main structure. The capacity of the factory is 400 movements per day, and 400 hands are employed.

THE PERRY MOVEMENT.

In 1886 Mr. John C. Dueber, of watch case fame, purchased a controlling interest in the Hampden Company. As the company had been behind in their orders and the movement had a good reputation, Mr. Dueber thought it would be wise to enlarge the works and make the output at least five hundred movements per day. With this object in view he visited several tracts of land in Springfield, but found that the only suitable land in that place, then on the

THE HAMPDEN WATCH FACTORY, AT SPRINGFIELD, MASS.

market, was held at such exorbitant figures that it was useless to spend further time there. Wishing to extend his case works at Newport, Ky., he thought it would be advisable to secure a desirable location and build new factories for both concerns in the same neighborhood, thus making the largest and most magnificent watch establishment in the world. Accordingly Mr. Dueber advertised for a location, and finally settled on Canton, Ohio, as the most appropriate place. The people of Canton donated $100,000 and

THE HAMPDEN WATCH FACTORY, AT CANTON, OHIO.

twenty acres of land for the factories. The site is at the western edge of the city, on a bluff with a commanding view. The illustration, made from the architect's plans, gives a fair idea of how the Hampden factory looks. The building for the Dueber factory is very similar in construction. The buildings are all three stories high, with pressed brick and cut stone fronts, and from right to left, occupy a frontage of 1,140 feet. In the rear of each building is a smaller line of buildings, not shown in the illustration. The engine and boiler rooms are also situated back of each building. The buildings were ready for occupancy in the spring of 1888, when the machinery was moved from Springfield.

Chas. D. Rood is President, Treasurer and Business Manager, and Henry J. Cain, Superintendent.

CHAPTER XVIII.

THE Waterbury Watch was invented to fill a demand for a cheap watch. The Waltham, Elgin and other companies manufactured watches that were within the reach of people of moderate means, but there still existed a wide field which was unoccupied until the Waterbury Watch made its appearance. There were still millions of people who could not afford to purchase a watch even at the low price at which the Waltham, Elgin, *et. al.* were selling. Some of the manufacturers of the Naugatuck Valley, appreciating this fact, undertook to fill this want, and their endeavors were crowned with success. The first thing required was a man who could make a model watch, that would possess fair qualifications as a time-keeper, and yet have a less number of parts than any watch then on the market. It was absolutely essential that it should possess a less number of parts than those then on the market, in order to cheapen its manufacture, so that the complete watch, case and all might be retailed at $3.50. The making of the model was intrusted to Mr. D. A. Buck, at that time a watchmaker of Worcester, Mass. Mr. Buck was of a mechanical turn of mind. At the Centennial Exhibition, in 1876, there was shown the largest steam engine in the world, and close to it was working its brother, the smallest. The small engine was designed and built by Mr. Buck, and in its construction he used only such tools as are usually found on a watch repairer's bench. This machine consisted of a boiler, an engine, with cylinder, governor, valves and all the details of its monster brother, worked to a charm, and was yet so small that it could be completely covered with an ordinary thimble. Mr. Buck's first experiment on the model proved a failure, but after a few months' work he produced a working model which was pronounced satisfactory. This model was shown to Mr. Charles Benedict, of the Benedict & Burnham Manufacturing Co., of Waterbury, Conn., who after testing it in various ways pronounced it satisfactory, and made arrangements for starting the work of manufacture in his establishment. It was supposed that with the tools owned by the Benedict & Burnham Co., together with special tools to be manufactured, that the work could be commenced in about six months. This was in January, 1878, but it was not until December, 1879, that everything was ready for the start. The rooms set apart in the factory soon proved too small, and a special building was erected for the purpose. A stock company was incorporated under the style of "The Waterbury Watch Company," and Mr. Benedict was elected as the first President. The movement was patented, and the

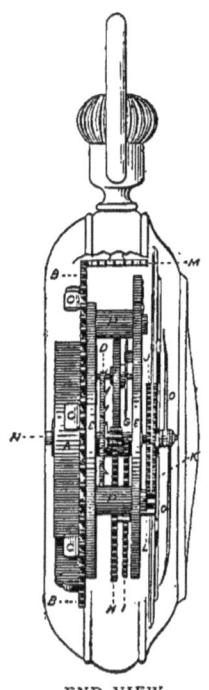

END VIEW.

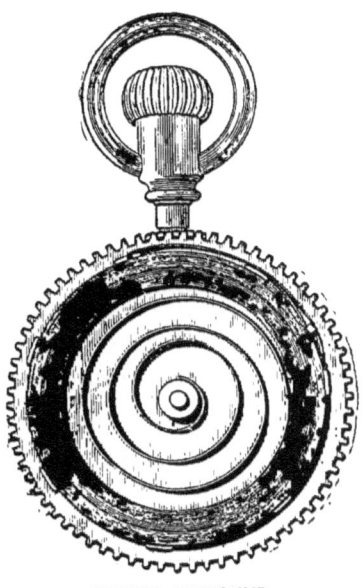

SPRING UNWOUND.

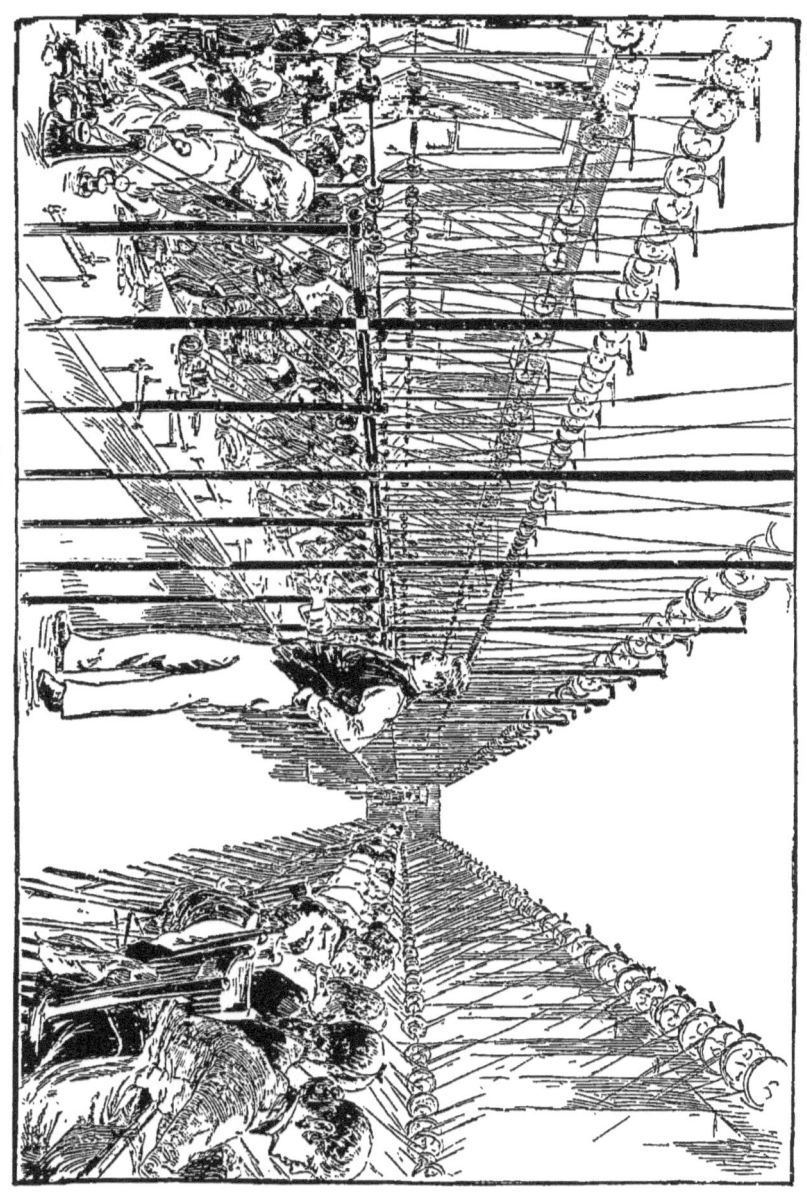

VIEW IN THE TRAIN ROOM OF THE WATERBURY FACTORY.

patents became the property of the company. The new factory was designed by Mr. H. W. Hartwell, of Boston, the architect of the Waltham and Elgin companies' factories. When the building was finished and furnished it was found that nearly half a million of dollars had been expended.

The first few thousand movements were placed in colored celluloid cases, but these were soon abandoned for a nickel-silver case. The first watches had open dials through which the working parts could be seen, but this was soon changed for a full dial and solid plates. The Waterbury Watch is novel in construction, and it is this novelty that admits of its being made and sold at a very low price. It is a stem winder, and takes a long time to wind owing to the extreme length of the spring, which in fact nearly fills the entire back of the case. The spring is wound upon a brass plate having a geared edge, and upon the stem is a smaller gear fitting into the larger, so that in winding the entire plate bearing the spring is made to revolve. This, however, is an old feature, but the novelty consists in the works themselves which are free to revolve upon the central axis, making an entire revolution every hour.

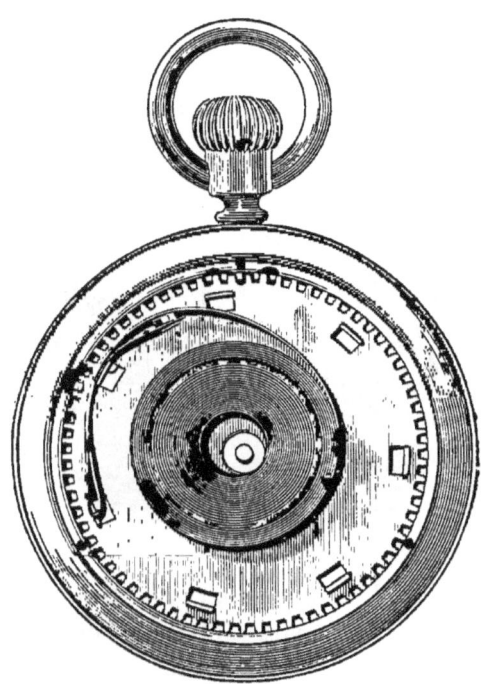

SPRING WOUND-UP.

It must be admitted, even by the most prejudiced, that the Waterbury is simplicity itself. The minute hand turns with the movement, and the hour hand is made to revolve by a train of three wheels, a hair spring and balance, and the movement is complete. Taking every part—screws, case, pinions, wheels, springs, in fact everything—and you have only fifty-eight parts in all. There are no jewels, the manufacturers claiming that the bearings being constantly changed by its peculiar motion, jewels are unnecessary.

THE WATERBURY FACTORY.

The factory, which is located at Waterbury, Conn., is a brick building and consists of three parts; a square central building four stories high, a long wing in the rear three stories high, and a smaller wing one story high. The spring department and pattern shop are located in the basement of the central building; the officers of the company occupy the first floor; the material room, designing room and rooms of the mechanical superintendent and draughtsman occupy the second floor; the finishing room occupies the fourth floor. The machine shop is located on the first floor of the wing, the case department on the second and train room on the third floor. This company gives employment to three hundred people and turns out fifteen hundred watches per day.

The present officers are: Charles Dickinson, President and Treasurer; Edward A. Locke, Secretary; George Merritt, Gen. Agent.

CHAPTER XIX.

THE Independent Watch company of Fredonia, N. Y. was organized in April 1880, by E. D. and C. M. Howard. The Howard Bros., for some years previous to this date, sold large numbers of watches on the installment plan. These watches, which were engraved "Independent Watch Co.," were manufactured for them by several American companies. The Howards decided, that as they used large numbers of watches, it would be policy to start a factory of their own.

The capital stock of the company was $150,000. E. D. Howard was elected President, E. S. Gates, Vice President and O. R. Burchard, Secretary and Treasurer. C. M. Howard was made business manager. The Board of Directors consisted of E. D. and C. M. Howard, W. H. Smith, O. R. Burchard, D. R. Barker and E. S. Gates. A building owned by the Howard Bros., was remodeled to serve as a factory. The machinery used in the factory, was for the most part a miscellaneous collection which had been purchased by the Howard Bros., from the assignees of several defunct companies. Portions of this machinery came from the old Cornell factory at Grand Crossing, Ill., while other portions came from the old United States factory at Marion, N. J. Considerable unfinished material had also been purchased by the Howard Bros., from the assignee of the United States Watch Company. This material, together with the machinery was sold to the new company, the Howard Bros., taking stock for it, in the new company.

Chas. S. Moseley was engaged as Superintendent, Jas. Dangerfield as foreman of the screw, plate and flat steel departments, John Baxter, foreman of escapement making. G. D. Parsons, foreman of jeweling and motion, and Thos. Perkins, foreman of finishing. The company first devoted their attention to the finishing up of the old United States movements. These movements however did not sell readily to the trade, and in 1882 a new 18-size model was made.

The company had sometime previous to this abandoned the idea of selling the movements at retail, and were confining their sales exclusively to the trade. Mr. Moseley was succeeded in Oct., 1881, by Jas. Dangerfield, under whose superintendency the new movements were gotten out, making their appearance in the summer of 1883.

A prejudice in the trade, existed against the watch, owing to the former methods adopted by the Howard Bros., in disposing of their watches, and this prejudice was so strong that it was found almost next to an impossibility to sell them.

In the fall of 1883, C. M. Howard went to Chicago to meet J. C. Adams and induce him, if possible, to associate himself with the company. After considering several propositions made by Mr. Howard, Mr. Adams finally went to Fredonia and examined the machinery, stock of movements, etc. He found that the company had on hand about eight thousand finished movements, and about two thousand more in a partially finished condition. The movements were anything but satisfactory, as the escapements were faulty and the general finish poor. Mr. Adams advised the company to finish up what movements they had in process of construction, sell them at any price they could get for them and close the factory temporarily in order to overhaul the machinery which was in a miserable condition. He also advised them to re-organize the company under a new name and expend several thousand dollars in new machiney, which was badly needed. This the company decided to do and accordingly they re-organized under the title of the Fredonia Watch Company, with a capital of $150,000.

Mr. Adams then made arrangements with the company to go on the road and in a few months he disposed of all of the old movements at a general average of six dollars each, which was considered a very good price for them.

During the year 1884, the machinery was thoroughly overhauled and some new and improved machinery and tools added. The factory was then started up again. Still the movements did not sell as well as they might and during the summer of 1885 the advisability of moving the factory to some other city, where capital could be interested, was thoroughly discussed.

Accordingly Mr. Adams was authorized to look up a new location and interest capital and organize a new company. He visited Peoria, Ill., and finally succeeded in opening negotiations which resulted in the sale of the machinery to a new company known as the Peoria Watch Company.

CHAPTER XX.

IN the fall of 1879, E. F. Bowman, then a retail jeweler, but now of the jobbing firm of Bowman & Musser, Lancaster, Pa., ordered a small outfit of watchmaking machinery from Geo. E. Hart, of Newark, N. J. This machinery he set up on the floor over his jewelry store, where he proposed to manufacture watches in a small way. In January, 1880, he engaged the services of W. H. Todd, who had formerly been superintendent of the Lancaster Watch Company, and had been succeeded by C. S. Moseley. Mr. Todd immediately proceeded to make a model watch. This being completed he busied himself in making some necessary small tools and then proceeded with the making of the watches. There were but five workmen in all, but they accomplished a great deal in a small space of time, for in 1882 some thirty complete watches were ready, while others were nearly finished.

THE BOWMAN WATCH.

The entire movement, with the exception of the balance and dial was made in the factory. These movements were all 16-size, nickel, stem wind, full jeweled, three-quarter plate, and were very handsome and well finished. The movements being manufactured on so small a scale were necessarily very expensive to produce and but little margin was left after selling, for the manufacturer. In the meantime Mr. Bowman had embarked in the wholesale jewelry trade and this business becoming pressing and occupying the greater part of his time, he decided that it would be policy to sell the watch plant if he could find a purchaser.

This was in the spring of 1882, and in the following summer a sale was effected to J. P. Stevens, of Atlanta, Ga. Mr. Stevens had for some time prior to this date been purchasing partially finished movements from the Hampden Watch Company and having his own workmen finish them, fitting a regulator of his own device and several other improvements.

After the purchase of this machinery Mr. Stevens organized a company known as the J. P. Stevens Watch Company, with a capital of $100,000. J. P. Stevens was elected President, and L. O. Stevens, Secretary. A new building was erected and additional machinery added to the plant. W. H. Todd was engaged as Superintendent and he made the model for the new watch, which closely resembled the Bowman movement. In the spring of 1884, C. L. Hoyt was made Superintenbent and Mr. Todd took charge of the train and plate department, C. H. Bagley, foreman escapement and jeweling, and T. W. Thompson, foreman of finishing.

Everything appeared to be going along smoothly, the factory turning out about ten movements per day, when in the fall of 1885, J. C. Freeman, the largest stockholder in the company died. After his death his heirs became involved in law suits and things assumed such a disagreeable phase that the Stevens brothers sold out their interest in the factory to the Freeman heirs. The new company was known as D. N. Freeman & Co. This company failed early in 1887 and the watch machinery was disposed of.

CHAPTER XXI.

THE Columbus Watch Company was organized Nov. 18, 1882, with a capital of $150,000, which was subsequently increased to $200,000. This company succeeded the firm of Gruen & Savage, who made a business of importing partially made Swiss movements and finishing them in Columbus. Messrs. Gruen & Savage occupied a two story brick factory built by them in 1879, which was purchased by the new company and a new building 35x95 feet was built on and connected by a passage-way with engine house in the rear as shown in the engraving. About the first step that the new company took was the making of tools and machinery for the manufacture of the watch complete. The tools and models for the first movements were completed in about nine months from the time of the organization of the company, being the quickest time on record. The company manufacture four sizes of movements, sixteen, eighteen, four and six sizes. They make both key and stem wind movements. The officers of the company are: D. Gruen, President and General Manager, and W. J. Savage, Secretary and Treasurer; Walter W. Owens,

THE COLUMBUS WATCH.

Supt. Three hundred hands are employed, and the output is about one hundred and fifty finished movements per day.

The various departments of the factory are presided over as follows: The escapement, screw and flat steel, John Walsh; pinion roughing and pinion cutting, W. C. Herman; pinion finishing, Wm. Keene; balance, W. Clarke; jeweling and motion, F. Bergmann; stem wind, Wm. Sauer; dial, W. Sherwood; adjusting, H. Ziplinski; finishing, H. Devitt.

The main offices of the Company are located at Columbus, Ohio, and 43 Maiden Lane, New York. The goods manufactured by this company bear an excellent reputation as time-keepers and sell readily.

THE FACTORY OF THE COLUMBUS WATCH COMPANY AT COLUMBUS, O.

CHAPTER XXII.

IN June, 1883, the Aurora Watch Company, of Aurora, Ill., was incorporated, with a capital stock of $250,000 in shares of $100 each. The projectors of the company had in view an idea which had been advanced on several occasions, but had never come to a successful issue, *i. e.*, a strictly trade watch company, or in other words, a company whose products should be controlled by the retail trade, doing away with the middle-man or jobber. The capital stock of this company is largely owned and controlled by retail dealers, who handle the product. One dealer only in each town is allowed the privilege of selling their goods, preference being given to the dealers who are stockholders.

The incorporators were E. W. Trask, A. Somarindyck, F. L. Pond, H. H. Evans, D. F. Van Liew, H. Miller, and A. J. Hopkins. The first officers were E. W. Trask, President; Albert H. Pike, Vice-President; Maurice Wendell, Treasurer and Business Manager; Geo. F. Johnson, Superintendent. The first directors were M. Huffman, E. W. Trask, A. H. Pike, Maurice Wendell, and Geo. F. Johnson. In March, 1885, Maurice Wendell was succeeded as

THE AURORA WATCH.

THE FACTORY OF THE AURORA WATCH COMPANY, AT AURORA, ILL.

Treasurer and Manager by A. Somarindyck, and shortly after Mr. Trask resigned as President, and was succeeded by Mr. A. Somarindyck. In December, 1885, G. F. Johnson was succeeded as superintendent by J. W. Hurd, who was succeeded by Robert McIntosh, who held the position till March 1, 1887, when Geo. F. Johnson, who planned and built the factory and its machinery, was reinstated as Superintendent and now holds that important position.

The illustration of the factory here given is from the architect's plans, the building at present not being complete. The one wing now occupied covers 135 x 35 feet, and is three stories and basement. The machinery building is 35 x 95 feet, with wing for boiler and engine room 25 x 40 feet. Some 200 hands are employed, and the capacity is 100 movements per day. The Aurora watches, which have good reputations as time-keepers, are made in various grades, and fit Elgin-style cases. They are full-plate, 18-size, nickel and gilt, with quick train.

The present officers of the company are A. Somarindyck, President; M. Huffman, Vice-President; J. H. Weber, Manager; N. Somarindyck, Treasurer; T. H. Day, Secretary, and Geo. F. Johnson, Superintendent.

The foremen of the various departments are as follows: Pinion finishing, Clarence Coonradt; pinion roughing, Henry Ulreci; jeweling, J. W. Morse; escapement, George Allspach; balance and screw, Robt. Shepard; damaskeening, E. D. Hanchett; gilding, Jno. Fairchild; finishing, C. H. Connor; plate, Eugene Spalding; machine shop, A. H. Clavois.

CHAPTER XXIII.

THE New Haven Watch Company was incorporated October, 13, 1883, with a capital of $100,000. W. E. Doolittle, who is the patentee of a movement was the organizer of the company. New Haven, Conn., was decided on as a site and work was at once commenced on the machinery. A two story brick building, formerly occupied as a machine shop, was rented January 1, 1884, and the machinery was moved into it. It was at first intended to manufacture the Doolittle watch, but the plan was abandoned and a regular lever watch substituted in its stead.

The first board of Directors consisted of Aaron Carter, Lewis J. Mulford, Gerritt S. Glenn, W. E. Doolittle, and J. H. Brewer. The first officers were: Aaron Carter, President; Lewis J. Mulford, Vice-President and Treasurer, and Gerritt S. Glenn, Secretary. In the fall of 1885, (the capital of the company being nearly exhausted), it became necessary to increase the working capital, and accordingly Mr. Brewer paid a visit to Trenton with the intention of interesting capitalists. His efforts were successful, as the Trenton people agreed to furnish the necessary capital should the factory be moved to their city. About three acres of land were purchased in Chambersburg, a suburb, and the erection of a factory immediately commenced. The capital was then increased to $250,000, the name changed to The Trenton Watch Company, and a new Board of Directors consisting of J. H. Brewer, W. F. Van Camp, T. W. Burger, Saml. K. Wilson, J. L. Murphy,

Lawrence Farrell and W. S. Stryker was elected. J. H. Brewer was elected President; W. F. Van Camp, Treasurer, and J. C. Thomas, Secretary. The people of Trenton subscribed $50,000 to the enterprise.

S. T. J. Byam, for many years with the American Waltham Watch Company and later with the Waterbury Watch Company was made Superintendent, a position which he still holds. F. W. Keegan, formerly with the Marion, Cheshire, and Waterbury companies, has charge of the finishing department. P. W. Brady, who was for twenty-five years connected with the American Waltham Watch Company, has charge of the train room. Charles Taylor, formerly with the American Waltham and Waterbury companies, has charge of the escapement room. A. E. Wait, formerly of Waltham, has charge of the machine shop, and E. A. Hitchcock has charge of the case making.

THE TRENTON MOVEMENT.

The factory, which is built of pressed brick, is one of the most complete in all its details. The finishing is all done in hard pine and the light is splendid, each workman having a window to himself. It is a three story and basement building, 50 x 55 feet, with a wing 34 x 120 feet.

The Trenton Watch is straight-line lever escapement, with second hand, 18-size, jeweled, stem wind and set, and quick train. The company make all their own cases which are known as "silverine." About 200 employees are now at work and the output is at present about 180 per day.

The full capacity of the factory is 500 finished watches per day with 250 hands. The present capital of the company is $300,000. For the first three years the company sold their movements direct to the retail trade but later on their product was handled by jobbers. The main office is situated at Trenton, N. J., and Francis E. Morse & Co., Chicago, are the sole western agents.

CHAPTER XXIV.

CHARLES S. MOSELEY, whose name has been intimately connected with the history of nearly every watch factory in this country, was born in Westfield, Mass., Feb. 28, 1828. In 1836 he accompanied his father to Princeton, Ill., but soon returned to Massachusetts. At the age of eighteen he entered a machine shop in Westfield, and some time afterwards went to Boston where he worked for George H. Fox, as a machinist, and remained there for some years. His first connection with the watch factories was in 1852, when he entered the employ of Dennison, Howard & Davis, who were then beginning the manufacture of watches in Roxbury, Mass. Mr. Moseley went with them when the factory was removed to Waltham, and remained with the company, serving in the capacity of foreman of the machine shop and later as master mechanic.

About the year 1859 the Nashua Watch Company was started, and Mr. Moseley cast his lot with it, acting as master mechanic. He designed and built the machinery with which that movement was manufactured; and it is worthy of remark, that no better watch has ever been made since in this country.

In the fall of 1864 Mr. Moseley identified himself with the Elgin National Watch Company, then just starting, and was made general superintendent, in which capacity he remained with the company till 1877.

Mr. Moseley has assisted, when they were in need of engineering help, a number of other factories. As a mechanical engineer and a designer of watch machinery especially, he has had no superiors and but few equals. Many well known inventions are due to his genius. Among those that have acquired a world wide reputation, we may mention the interchangeable stem wind mechanism of the Elgin National Watch Company, patented in 1876. The dust band, or dust excluder, used by the same company, the best and cheapest ever made. The triangular hair spring stud. A patent regulator, and many others. One of his earliest inventions in connection with the manufacture of watches is the spring or split chuck, an accessory now become universal and indispensible to every watch maker in the land.

At this writing, although somewhat advanced in years, Mr. Moseley is still actively engaged in mechanical engineering of an advanced nature, the full history and value of which must be reserved for future historians to chronicle.

P. S. Bartlett, whose name is familiar to every watchmaker and jeweler in America, and we might say the world, was born in Amesbury, Mass., September 3, 1834. His first connection with watch making, was in 1854 when he went to work for the Boston Watch Company, just after its removal to Waltham, Mass., where he occupied the position of foreman of the plate and screw department. In 1859 the American Watch Company put upon the market a new 18-size movement which they engraved "P. S. Bartlett" in honor of the subject of this sketch. In 1861 the same company manufactured their first ladies' watch which they also designated as the "P. S. Bartlett," having abandoned the 18-size made in 1859.

In 1864 he visited Chicago, and together with Messrs. Chas. S. Moseley, J. C. Adams, and Ira G. Blake, organ-

CHARLES S. MOSELEY.

ized the National Watch Company, of Chicago, afterwards known as the Elgin National Watch Company. He subsequently signed a contract with that company for five years as foreman of the plate and screw departments. He was for seven years assistant superintendent and general traveling agent for the company, during which time he introduced the Elgin Watches in Europe, selling them in Moscow, St. Petersburg and other cities. He is now in the wholesale and retail watch and jewelry business in Elgin.

CHAPTER XXV.

THE Cheshire Watch Company was incorporated in October, 1883, with a capital of $100,000. The company was organized by Messrs. A. E. Hotchkiss and Geo. J. Capewell, of Cheshire, Conn., who interested capitalists in the scheme. The first officers were Geo. J. Capewell, President, and E. R. Brown, Secretary and Treasurer. The

THE FACTORY OF THE CHESHIRE WATCH COMPANY, CHESHIRE, CONN.

factory is located at Cheshire and is a very handsome building 200 feet in length and 30 feet wide. The model for the Cheshire was made by Mr. D. A. Buck, the gentleman who made the original Waterbury model. This movement is so familiar to the trade that a description is unnecessary. In February, 1885, Mr. Brown was succeeded as

Secretary and Treasurer by Mr. N. Brigham Hall, who still occupies that position. Mr. Capewell resigned his position as President in July, 1886, and was succeeded by Mr. John Pearce. Mr. Buck retained the position of Superintendent until October, 1885.

The capital stock of the company is at present $250,000, and the product 150 watches per day. The factory has a capacity of 225 movements per day. The main office of the company is situated at Cheshire, Conn., with a branch office at 178 Broadway, New York. The present Superintendent is Henry Aehl, and the foremen of the various departments are as follows: Foreman machine department Paul Simon; plate, F. L. Wilkinson; gilding, H. Martin; pinion, G. S. Kendrick; pinion cutting and finishing, W. S. Welton; jeweling, C. Narthrop; motion, F. S. Brockett; stem wind, Joseph Jenkins; escapement, C. S. Guernsey; timing, Wm. Davis; finishing, Thos. Baker; case-room, W. E. Garde; buff-room, Orrin Hitchcock.

THE CHESHIRE WATCH.

The Manhattan Watch Company was organized in 1883 with a capital of $100,000. The company was organized mainly through the efforts of A. O. Jennings, who was formerly manager of the Jerome Clock Company. The factory of the company is located at 158 Monroe Street, New York City, and the offices of the company are at 235 Broadway.

In 1886 the capital of the company was increased to $150,000. The movements which the company manufacture are all 18-size, both open-face and hunting. They munufacture all their own cases. The company are now manufacturing one thousand watches per week and employ eighty-five hands. The officers of the company are A. O. Jennings, President; T. B. Jennings, Vice President; P. R. Jennings, Secretary and F. L. Park, Treasurer; R. G. Jennings is Superintendent.

CHAPTER XXVI.

HERMAN VON DER HEYDT, a native of Weisbaden, Germany, came to this country in 1881. He was a thorough machanic, having mastered the trade of watchmaker in one of the technical schools for which his country is justly famous. He located in Chicago and soon after started the manufacture of a self-winding watch. He succeeded in his object in 1883. This movement he patented Feb. 19, 1884. In all he has manufactured but thirty-four movements, five of which were full nickel and the balance gilt. This watch, which is peculiar in mechanism, might be termed a full-plate. It is 18-size, lever escapement and full jeweled. The winding mechanism is of the gravity variety, consisting of a somewhat heavy steel crescent, which by the motion of the body moves up and down and is connected to a ratchet on the winding arbor.

THE SELF-WINDING WATCH.

The small number of watches made is accounted for by the fact that they were all hand made, the inventor having only at his disposal an American lathe, a heavy lathe with universal head and the usual outfit of watch repairer's tools. Even then he manufactured the watches piece-meal taking only such time as he could spare from his regular business as jeweler and watch repairer. The watches were all sold as fast as manufactured, the gilt movements bringing $75 and the nickel ones $90 each. Mr. Von der Heydt has had several flattering offers made him by watch companies and wealthy jewelers but has always declined, preferring to manufacture the movements himself without aid at such times as he could get to work on them. They are finely finished and keep excellent time.

The United States Watch Company, of Waltham, Mass., was incorporated in July, 1884, with a capital of $50,000. The stockholders of the company were Chas. V. Woerd, who had been connected with the American Waltham Watch Company for twenty-five years, E. C. Hammer, T. B. Eaton and Nutting Bros., of Waltham. The Nutting Bros. and Mr. Woerd were associated in business under the name of the Waltham Watch Tool Company. The officers of the company are T. B. Eaton, President, and E. C. Hammer, Treasurer. The company purchased a tract of land and built a small factory, into which the tools, manufactured previously by the Waltham Watch Tool Company, were moved.

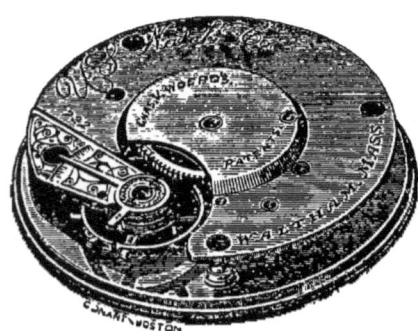
THE UNITED STATES WATCH.

Mr. Woerd made a model for a 16-size, three-quarter plate watch, having a dome in the centre, in order to accommodate the center wheel, as the barrel was so wide that no room was left for it. This watch was a stem-wind, the mechanism of which was patented by Mr. Woerd. Some three thousand of these movements had been made, up to the fall of 1887, but they had met with a poor sale, as the movement required a special case.

In November, 1887, Mr. Woerd severed his connection with the company. The capital stock of the company was increased to $150,000 and work commenced on a new model which was a 16-size, three-quarter plate, quick train, with lever escapement, and expansion balance. Like the first it was stem wind, using the same machinism, but the wide barrel was done away with, thus rendering the dome for center wheel unnecessary. As these watches are not yet on the market it is impossible to say how they will be received by the trade.

CHAPTER XXVII.

IN the summer of 1885, J. C. Adams visited Peoria, Ill., to interest the capitalists of that city in a watch factory enterprize, as described in Chapter XIX. As a result of his arguments Messrs. E. F. Baldwin, Albert Truesdale, J. C. Woelfle, J. L. Flinn, Eustis H. Smith and Fredk. Eynatten, all citizens of Peoria, went to Fredonia in the fall of 1885 and inspected the factory. Negotiations were entered into, which resulted in the sale of the factory to the Peoria Watch Company, which was incorporated Dec. 19, 1885, with a capital of $250,000. $150,000 in money, notes and stock was paid for the Fredonia plant. A building was started in Peoria in March 1886, and completed in the following June, when the Fredonia machinery was moved into it.

The old Fredonia model was altered over to meet the requirements of a quick-train, railroad watch, 18-size and fifteen jeweled. Mr. Adams then went on the road and made several very heavy contracts for the company with western railroads. In the summer of 1887, Mr. Adams had sold so many movements that the company was some six weeks to two months behind with its orders. Complaints began to come in that the movements were being neglected, that the escapement was faultly and the finish poor. The superintendent then in charge, G. P. Benezet sent in his resignation and Ferd. F. Ide of Springfield, Ill., was appointed superintendent. Mr. Adams severed his connection with the company April 14, 1888.

The company employs about ninety hands and the product is about thirty movements per day. These movements are all nameless and are known as Grade A, No. 1 special, Grade C, Grade D, Grade A. & K., and numbers one to six inclusive. They are all 18-size, fifteen jeweled, quick train.

THE FACTORY OF THE PEORIA WATCH COMPANY, AT PEORIA, ILL.

At present the officers of the company are: Eustis H. Smith, President; W. H. Smith, Treasurer; W. W. Hammond, Secretary; J. B. Greenhut, Vice President; and Clarence M. Howard, Manager. The directors are W. W. Hammond, E. S. Smith, J. B. Greenhut, W. H. Smith, J. C. Woelfle, C. R. Wheeler and C. M. Howard. Ferd. F. Ide is superintendent and the foremen of the various departments are as follows: T. M. Younglove, jeweling; W. Earler, damas-

keening; D. R. Buchanan, dial; E. F. French, plate room;
F. A. A. Hordon, gilding; J. Frazier, engraving; J. H.
Burns, train room; F. S. Wenk, balances; W. H. H. Murray, escapement, flat steel and screw; M. Clapp, adjusting
and J. B. Wormwood, machine shop.

The Seth Thomas Clock Company started the manufacture of watches in 1883. During that year an addition was made to their clock factory, and the tools and machinery previously made and purchased were moved into it. The first watches were placed on the market in 1885, and were 18-size, three-quarter plate, open face and stem-wind. The model for this movement was made by Herman Reinicke, who acted as master watchmaker for the company until the spring of 1886 when he was succeeded by Chas. L. Higginbottom. Under Mr. Higginbottom's administration a new movement

THE SETH THOMAS WATCH.

was turned out, it being a hunting case movement with a different stem-wind mechanism from the original and quick train. The company are now turning out one hundred movements per day, and employ two hundred hands. Four grades of hunting and open face movements are made, and additions will be made to this line as rapidly as possible.

The New York Standard Watch Company put its first product on the market in the fall of 1887. This movement, which is an 18-size, full plate, straight line, lever-worm, escapement, stem-wind and open face, is novel in construction. The office of the company is situated at 83 Nassau Street and the factory is at Jersey City, N. J. H. B. Claflin & Co., New York, have recently been appointed as wholesale selling agents for the company.

THE NEW YORK STANDARD WATCH.

The Wichita Watch Company was organized and incorporated in July 1887, with a capital stock of $250,000. The officers are J. R. Sniveley, President, H. W. Lewis, Treasurer and Irvin Stratton, Secretary. The company immediately made preparations for building a factory. The building which was finished June 1st, 1888, is a substantial structure built of light colored limestone, taken from an adjacent quarry. It consists of a central building 44 x 54 feet with a wing each side 148 x 30 feet. The central structure is four stories in height while the wings are three stories. The engine house is situated immediately back of the central structure. This building has a capacity for working six hundred hands and turning out from one hundred and fifty to two hundred watches per day. On both ends of the building are situated tower-like structures which are fire escapes. These towers contain winding stair cases, built of iron and are accessible from each floor through iron doors. The watch which the company proposes to manufacture is an 18-size, half plate, adjusted and full jeweled and made to fit any American case. No machinery has yet been placed in the factory although the engine is already in place and boilers in. It is not definitely known when operations will be commenced.

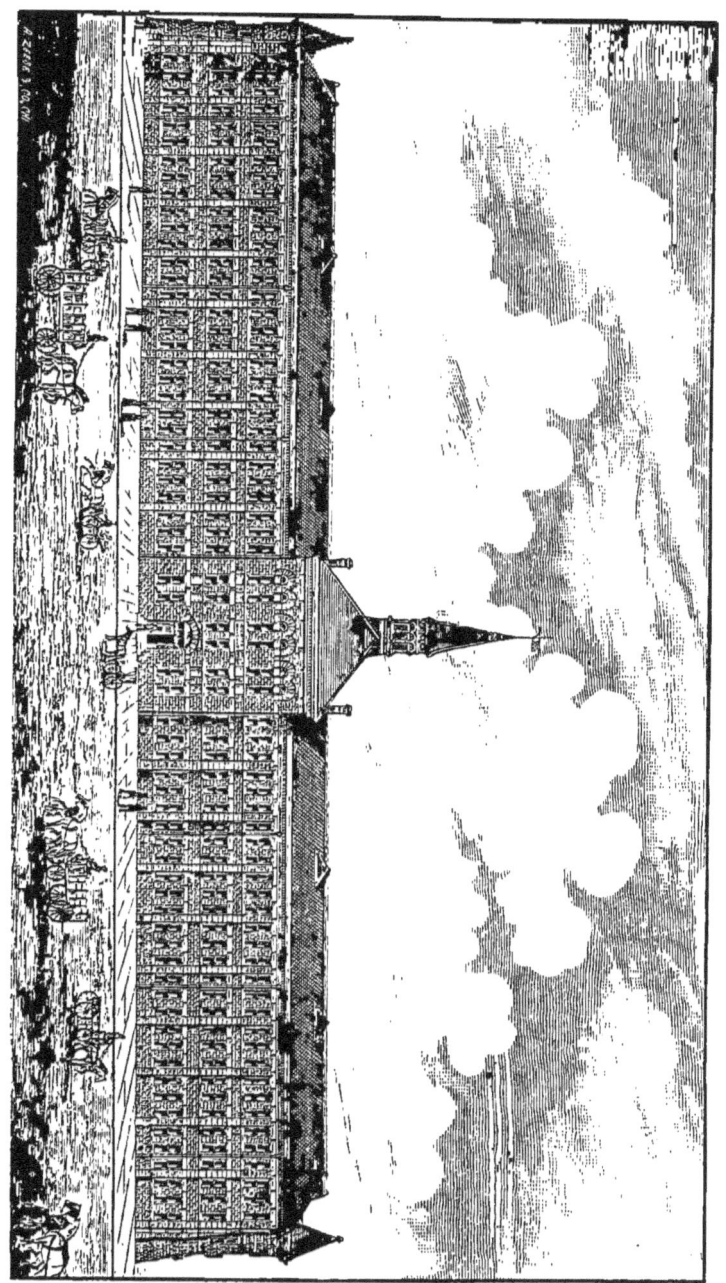

THE FACTORY OF THE WICHITA WATCH COMPANY, WICHITA, KAS.

www.ingramcontent.com/pod-product-compliance
Lightning Source LLC
Chambersburg PA
CBHW030117170426
43198CB00009B/645